Study Guide

Charles Beem

Business Essentials

Seventh Edition

Ronald J. Ebert
Ricky W. Griffin

Upper Saddle River, New Jersey 07458

Editor-in-Chief: Natalie E. Anderson
AVP/Executive Editor: Jodi McPherson
Editorial Project Manager: Kristin Kaiser, KMK Editorial Services
Production Project Manager: Lynne Breitfeller
Operations Specialist: Natacha Moore

10 9 8 7 6 5 4 3 2 1

ISBN-13: 978-0-13-607850-0
ISBN-10: 0-13-607850-8

This study guide is dedicated to my beloved wife, Karen I. Beem, 12/06/1957–01/21/2006, Professor and Hospital Laboratory Supervisor.

CONTENTS

Chapter 1
The U.S. Business Environment

Think of this study guide as your tutor. It is designed to give you more practice and familiarity the with terminology and concepts discussed in the textbook. Be sure to read and study each chapter carefully before attempting these exercises. (Answers are found at the end of each chapter.)

Learning Objectives
After reading this chapter, you should be able to:

1. Define the nature of U.S. business and identify its main goals and functions.
2. Describe the external environments of business and discuss how these environments affect the success or failure of any organization.
3. Describe the different types of global economic systems according to the means by which they control the factors of production.
4. Show how markets, demand, and supply affect resource distribution in the United States.
5. Identify the elements of private enterprise and explain the various degrees of competition in the U.S. economic system.
6. Explain the importance of the economic environment to business and identify the factors used to evaluate the performance of an economic system.

True-False
Indicate whether the statement is generally true or false by placing a "T" or an "F" in the space provided. If it is a false statement, correct it so that it becomes a true statement.

_____ 1. The domestic business environment refers to the international forces that affect business.

_____ 2. An economic system is a nation's system for allocating its resources among its citizens, both individuals and organizations.

_____ 3. Physical resources are the intangible things that organizations use to conduct their business.

_____ 4. The economic system featuring characteristics of both planned and market economies is called a mixed market economy.

_____ 5. The law of supply indicates that the quantity supplied rises as the price falls.

_____ 6. A shortage will exist whenever the current price is above the market or equilibrium price.

_____ 7. When an industry has only a handful of sellers an oligopoly exists.

_____ 8. In monopolistic competition product differentiation gives sellers some control over prices.

_____ 9. The gross domestic product (GDP), refers to the total value of all goods and services produced within a given period by a national economy through domestic factors of production.

_____ 10. Inflation occurs when there are widespread price increases throughout an economic system.

_____ 11. A negative balance of trade results when a country exports more than it imports.

_____ 12. The government acts to manage the U.S. economic system through two sets of policies: physical and philosophical.

_____ 13. The government acts to manage the U.S. economic system through two sets of policies: fiscal and monetary.

Multiple Choice
Circle the best answer for each of the following questions.

1. The political-legal environment reflects the relationship between
    a. goods and services.
    b. capital and information resources.
    c. customers and suppliers.
    d. business and government.

2. The financial resources needed to start a business, operate it, and keep it growing is referred to as
    a. labor.
    b. capital.
    c. physical resources.
    d. information resources.

3. The process of converting government enterprises into privately owned companies is
    a. communism.
    b. Marxism and Maoism.
    c. privatization.
    d. socialism.

4. Capitalism is characterized by
    a. economic freedom and competition.
    b. public ownership over all productive resources.
    c. public ownership and operation of key industries.
    d. government control over prices and what is produced.

5. Which of the following is true concerning a market?
    a. Demand indicates that as the price goes up, sales increase.
    b. An equilibrium price exists when the quantity demanded equals the quantity supplied.
    c. Supply shows how much people will buy at various prices.
    d. If demand increases in a market, then the price of the product will likely fall.

6. Private enterprise found within market economies requires the presence of
    a. private property rights.   b. freedom of choice.
    c. profits and competition.   d. All of the above.

7. Perfect competition is a situation in which
    a. there are so many buyers and sellers that no single buyer or seller has the ability to influence market price.
    b. many sellers differentiate their products from their competitors in at least some small way.
    c. the market is dominated by a few sellers.
    d. the market is dominated by a single seller.

8. Which of the following is *true*?
    a. Successful product differentiation allows monopolistically competitive firms some control over the prices they charge.
    b. A natural monopoly exists when one company can most efficiently supply all the needed goods and services.
    c. In an oligopoly, a change in the price by one firm can significantly affect the sales of other firms.
    d. All of the above.

9. Which of the following comes closest to being a monopoly?
    a. A local cable television provider   b. A local grocery store
    c. An international airline company   d. A farmer

10. Perfect competition is characterized by
    a. firms selling differentiated products.
    b. buyers and sellers unaware of the prices that others are paying and receiving in the marketplace.
    c. market prices set exclusively by supply and demand and accepted by both sellers and buyers.
    d. difficult entry and exit by firms.

11. The business cycle includes
    a.   patterns of short-term expansions and contractions in an economy.
    b.   national debt.
    c.   the balance of trade.
    d.   unemployment.

12. Which of the following is *false*?
    a.   A negative balance of trade (a trade deficit) means a country is exporting more than it is importing.
    b.   A budget deficit means the government is spending more money than it has collected in taxes, and this increases the country's national debt.
    c.   Fiscal policy is the manipulation of government spending and taxes.
    d.   Monetary policy is the manipulation of the nation's money supply in order to affect interest rates.

13. Which of the following measures the prices of typical products purchased by consumers living in urban areas?
    a.   Local stock portfolios   b.   Unemployment rates
    c.   Dow Jones Industrial Average   d.   Consumer price index (CPI)

14. Which of the following is NOT true?
    a.   A balance of trade is the value of all products *exported* minus the value of *imported* products. A *positive* balance results when a country exports (sells to other countries) more than it imports (buys from other countries).
    b.   A *negative* balance means that a country imports more than it exports.
    c.   A negative balance is also called a trade deficit.
    d.   The national debt is the amount of money that a government's creditors owe to it.

Match the Terms and Concepts with Their Definitions

a. business	q. socialism	gg. oligopoly
b. profits	r. demand	hh. monopoly
c. economic system	s. supply	ii. natural monopoly
d. factors of production	t. law of demand	jj. stability
e. labor (or human resources)	u. law of supply	kk. inflation
f. capital	v. demand and supply schedule	ll. depression
g. physical resources	w. demand curve	mm. unemployment
h. information resources	x. supply curve	nn. GNP
i. planned economy	y. market price	oo. real GDP
j. market economy	z. surplus	pp. GDP
k. market	aa. shortage	qq. productivity
l. external environment	bb. private enterprise	rr. recession
m. entrepreneur	cc. private property rights	ss. national debt

n.   capitalism
o.   mixed market economy
p.   privatization

dd. competition
ee. pure competition
ff. monopolistic competition

tt.   monetary policies
uu. fiscal policies

_____ 1.   Mechanism for exchange between buyers and sellers of a particular good or service.

_____ 2.   The funds needed to create and operate a business enterprise.

_____ 3.   The difference between a business's revenues and its expenses.

_____ 4.   An organization that provides goods and services to earn profits.

_____ 5.   A nation's system for allocating its resources among its citizens.

_____ 6.   An economy that relies on a centralized government to control all or most factors of production and to make all or most production and allocation decisions.

_____ 7.   An economy in which individuals control production and allocation decisions through supply and demand.

_____ 8.   Tangible things organizations use in the conduct of their business.

_____ 9.   Data and other information used by businesses.

_____ 10. The physical and mental capabilities of people as they contribute to economic production.

_____ 11. Resources used in the production of goods and services—natural resources, labor, capital, and entrepreneurs.

_____ 12. Everything outside an organization's boundaries that might affect it.

_____ 13. The process of converting government enterprises into privately owned companies.

_____ 14. The willingness and ability of buyers to purchase a good or service.

_____ 15. The willingness and ability of producers to offer a good or service for sale.

_____ 16. Principle that buyers will purchase (demand) more of a product as its price drops, and less as its price increases.

_____ 17. Principle that producers will offer (supply) more of a product for sale as its price rises, and less as its price drops.

_____ 18. Assessment of the relationship between demand and supply at different price levels.

_____ 19. A graph showing how many units of a product will be supplied (offered for sale) at different prices.

_____ 20. A graph showing how many units of a product will be demanded (bought) at different prices.

_____ 21. A planned economic system in which the government owns and operates only selected major sources of production.

_____ 22. An economic system featuring characteristics of both planned and market economies.

_____ 23. An individual who accepts the risks and opportunities involved in creating and operating a new business venture.

_____ 24. A market economy that provides for private ownership and encourages entrepreneurship by offering profits as an incentive.

_____ 25. An industry in which one company can most efficiently supply all needed goods and services.

_____ 26. A market or industry characterized by numerous buyers and relatively numerous sellers trying to differentiate their products from those of competitors.

_____ 27. A market or industry characterized by numerous small firms producing identical products.

_____ 28. A market or industry characterized by a handful of (generally large) sellers with the power to influence the prices of their products.

_____ 29. A market or industry in which there is only one producer, which can therefore set the prices of its products.

_____ 30. Vying among businesses for the same resources or customers.

_____ 31. A situation in which the quantity supplied exceeds the quantity demanded.

_____ 32. A situation in which the quantity demanded exceeds the quantity supplied.

_____ 33. The profit-maximizing price at which the quantity of goods demanded and the quantity of goods supplied are equal.

_____ 34. An economic system that allows individuals to pursue their own interests without undue governmental restriction.

_____ 35. The right to buy, own, use, and sell almost any form of property.

_____ 36. A particularly severe and long-lasting recession.

_____ 37. The level of joblessness among people actively seeking work.

_____ 38. The phenomenon of widespread price increases throughout an economic system.

_____ 39. The condition in which the balance between the money available in an economy and the goods produced in it is growing at about the same rate.

_____ 40. The value of all goods and services produced in a year by a nation's economy through domestic factors of production.

_____ 41. The value of all goods and services produced by an economic system in a year regardless of where the factors of production are located.

_____ 42. The gross domestic product adjusted for inflation and changes in the value of currency.

_____ 43. Government economic policies that determine the size of a nation's money supply.

_____ 44. Government economic policies that determine how the government collects and spends its revenues.

_____ 45. The total amount that a nation owes its creditors.

_____ 46. The economic period during which aggregate output, as measured by GDP, declines.

_____ 47. The measure of economic growth that compares how much a system produces with the resources needed to produce it.

Learning Objectives—Short Answer or Essay Questions

Learning Objective #1: Define the nature of U.S. business and identify its main goals and functions.

Learning Objective #2: Describe the external environments of business and discuss how these environments affect the success or failure of any organization.

Learning Objective #3: Describe the different types of global economic systems according to the means by which they control the factors of production.

Learning Objective #4: Show how markets, demand, and supply affect resource distribution in the United States.

Learning Objective #5: Identify the elements of private enterprise and explain the various degrees of competition in the U.S. economic system

Learning Objective #6: Explain the importance of the economic environment to business and identify the factors used to evaluate the performance of an economic system.

Critical Thinking Questions

1. Why should a large trade deficit concern the U.S. economy?

2. Describe how inflation can affect an economic system.

Brain Teaser

What factors could justify natural monopolies in an economic system?

ANSWERS

True-False—Answers

1. False: The domestic business environment refers to the environment in which a firm conducts its operations and derives its revenues.
2. True
3. False: Physical resources are the tangible things that organizations use to conduct their business.
4. True
5. False: The law of supply indicates that the quantity supplied rises as the price *rises*.
6. False: Whenever the current price is above the market or equilibrium price then a *surplus* exists.
7. True
8. True
9. True
10. True
11. False: A negative balance of trade results when a country imports more than it exports.
12. False: The government acts to manage the U.S. economic system through two sets of policies: fiscal and monetary. (There is a big difference between *fiscal* and *physical*.)
13. True

Multiple Choice—Answers

1. d	3. c	5. b	7. a	9. a	11. a	13. d
2. b	4. a	6. d	8. d	10. c	12. a	14. d

Match the Terms and Concepts with Their Definitions—Answers

1. k	8. g	15. s	22. o	29. hh	36. ll	43. tt
2. f	9. h	16. t	23. m	30. dd	37. mm	44. uu
3. b	10. e	17. u	24. n	31. z	38. kk	45. ss
4. a	11. d	18. v	25. ii	32. aa	39. jj	46. rr
5. c	12. l	19. x	26. ff	33. y	40. pp	47. qq
6. i	13. p	20. w	27. ee	34. bb	41. nn	
7. j	14. r	21. q	28. gg	35. cc	42. oo	

Learning Objectives—Short Answer or Essay Questions—Answers

Learning Objective #1: Define the nature of U.S. business and identify its main goals and functions.
Businesses are organizations that produce or sell goods or services to make a profit. *Profits* are the difference between a business's revenues and expenses. The prospect of earning profits encourages individuals and organizations to open and expand businesses. The benefits of business activities also extend to wages paid to workers and to taxes that support government functions.

Learning Objective #2: Describe the external environments of business and discuss how these environments affect the success or failure of any organization.
All businesses, regardless of their size, location, or mission, operate within a larger *external environment*. The external environment consists of everything outside an organization's boundaries that might affect it. It plays a major role in determining the success or failure of any organization. The external environment includes the following:

- The *domestic business environment* is the environment in which a firm conducts its operations and derives its revenues.
- The *global business environment* refers to the international forces that affect a business, including international trade agreements, international economic conditions, and political unrest.
- The *technological environment* includes all the ways by which firms create value for their constituents, including human knowledge, work methods, physical equipment, electronics and telecommunications, and various processing systems that are used to perform business activities.
- The *political-legal environment* reflects the relationship between business and government, usually in the form of government regulation of business.
- The *sociocultural environment* includes the customs, mores, values, and demographic characteristics of the society in which an organization functions. It determines the goods, services, and standards of business conduct that a society is likely to value and accept.
- The *economic environment* refers to relevant conditions that exist in the economic system in which a company operates.

Learning Objective #3: Describe the different types of global economic systems according to the means by which they control the factors of production.
An *economic system* is a nation's system for allocating its resources among its citizens. Economic systems differ in terms of who owns or controls the five basic *factors of production*: labor, capital, entrepreneurs, physical resources, and information resources. In *planned economies*, the government controls all or most factors. In *market economies*, which are based on the principles of *capitalism*, individuals and businesses control the factors of production. Most countries today have *mixed market economies* that are dominated by one of these systems but include elements of the other. The process of *privatization* is an important means by which many of the world's planned economies are moving toward mixed economic systems.

Learning Objective #4: Show how markets, demand, and supply affect resource distribution in the United States.
The U.S. economy is strongly influenced by markets, demand, and supply. *Demand* is the willingness and ability of buyers to purchase a good or service. *Supply* is the willingness and ability of producers to offer goods and services for sale. Demand and supply work together to set a *market* or *equilibrium price*—the price at which the quantity of goods demanded and the quantity of goods supplied are equal.

Learning Objective #5: Identify the elements of private enterprise and explain the various degrees of competition in the U.S. economic system.
The U.S. economy is founded on the principles of *private enterprise*: *private property rights*, *freedom of choice*, *profits*, and *competition*. Degrees of competition vary because not all industries are equally competitive. Under conditions of *pure competition*, numerous small firms compete in a market governed entirely by demand and supply. An *oligopoly* involves a handful of sellers only. A *monopoly* involves only one seller.

Learning Objective #6: Explain the importance of the economic environment to business and identify the factors used to evaluate the performance of an economic system.
The basic goals of an economic system are *economic stability* and *economic growth*. Measures of how well an economy has accomplished these goals include *gross national product*, *gross domestic product*, *productivity*, *balance of trade*, and *national debt*. To know how much standard of living is improving, we consider two factors: gross national product (GNP), which is the total value of all goods and services produced by a national economy within a given period *regardless of where the factors of production are located* and gross domestic product (GDP), which is the total value of all goods and services produced within a given period by a national economy *through domestic factors of production*. Nominal GDP means GDP measured in current dollars, but we calculate real GDP when we calculate GDP to account for *changes in currency values and price changes*. The U.S. government uses *fiscal policies* to manage the effects of its spending and revenue collection and *monetary policies* to control the size of the nation's money supply. *Stability* means that the amount of money available in a system and the quantity of goods and services produced in it are growing at about the same rate. Two key threats to stability include *inflation* (when prices increase throughout an economic system and purchasing power declines) and *unemployment* (the level of joblessness among people actively seeking work). When it's up, people have less purchasing power.

Critical Thinking Questions—Answers

1. **Why should a large trade deficit concern the U.S. economy?**
   Trade deficit affects economic growth because the amount of money spent on foreign products has not been paid in full. Therefore, it is, in effect, borrowed money, and borrowed money costs more in the form of interest. The money that flows out of the country to pay off the deficit can't be used to invest in productive enterprises, either at home or overseas.
2. **Describe how inflation can affect an economic system.**
   Inflation occurs when an economic system experiences widespread price increases. Instability results when the amount of money injected into an economy exceeds the increase in actual output, so people have more to spend but the same quantity of products available to buy. As supply and demand principles tell us, as people compete with one another to buy available products, prices go up. These high prices will eventually bring the amount of money in the economy back down. However, these processes are imperfect—the additional money will not be distributed proportionately to all people, and price increases often continue beyond what is really necessary. As a result, purchasing power for many people declines.

Brain Teaser—Answer

What factors could justify natural monopolies in an economic system?

Natural monopolies are industries in which one company can most efficiently supply all needed goods or services. Many electric companies are natural monopolies because they can supply all the power needed in a local area. Duplicate facilities—such as two power plants and two sets of power lines—would be inefficient.

Chapter 2
Business Ethics and Social Responsibility

Learning Objectives
After reading this chapter, you should be able to:

1. Explain how individuals develop their personal codes of ethics and why ethics are important in the workplace.
2. Distinguish social responsibility from ethics, identify organizational stakeholders, and characterize social consciousness today.
3. Show how the concept of social responsibility applies both to environmental issues and to a firm's relationships with its customers, employees, and investors.
4. Identify four general approaches to social responsibility and describe the four steps that a firm must take to implement a social responsibility program.
5. Explain how issues of social responsibility and ethics affect small businesses.

True-False
Indicate whether the statement is generally true or false by placing a "T" or an "F" in the space provided. If it is a false statement, correct it so that it becomes a true statement.

_____ 1. Each person's personal code of ethics is determined by a combination of factors that are formed and refined throughout the person's lifetime.

_____ 2. Global standards provide a framework for ethical business practices.

_____ 3. Using advertising to project a green image without adopting substantive environmentally friendly changes is consumerism.

_____ 4. One of the most common approaches to formalizing ethical business practices within an organization is to start with top management support.

_____ 5. Determining what is right in any given situation can be difficult.

_____ 6. By law, businesses cannot discriminate against people in any facet of the employment relationship.

_____ 7. Most companies that strive to be responsible to their stakeholders concentrate first and foremost on five main groups: *customers, employees, investors, suppliers*, and their *local communities*.

15

_____ 8.   Price gouging is using confidential information to gain from the purchase or sale of stocks.

_____ 9.   Firms with the highest degree of social responsibility exhibit the accommodative stance.

_____ 10. The first step in assessing ethical behavior is to analyze the facts to determine the most appropriate moral values.

_____ 11. The lowest level of social responsibility is the proactive stance.

_____ 12. Individual values and codes are the standards of behavior that guide individual managers in their work.

_____ 13. Consumers have the right to fair prices, the right to good service, the right to complain, and the right to return unused products for a full refund.

_____ 14. Consumerism was a movement that began in the 1960s and was designed to protect the rights of consumers in their dealings with businesses.

_____ 15. Collusion occurs when two or more firms agree to collaborate on such wrongful acts as price fixing.

_____ 16. In recent years, increased attention has been given to ethics in advertising and product information.

_____ 17. Whistle-blowing occurs when an employee who detects and tries to put an end to a company's unethical, illegal, or socially irresponsible actions publicizes them.

_____ 18. Investors can be cheated in many ways, but most scams fall into two categories: (1) misrepresenting company resources and (2) diverting earnings or assets so that the investor's rightful return is reduced.

_____ 19. A utility norm occurs when an activity may benefit the individual to the detriment of his or her employer.

_____ 20. Managers must take steps to foster companywide philosophies of social responsibility and ethics.

Multiple Choice
Circle the best answer for each of the following questions.

1. Which of the following is one of the steps suggested in the textbook for applying ethical judgments to situations that may arise during the course of business?
    a. Gather the relevant factual information.
    b. Determine the most appropriate moral values.
    c. Make an ethical judgment based on the rightness and wrongness of the proposed activity or policy.
    d. All of the above.

2. Which of the following is NOT one of the steps in assessing ethical behavior?
    a. Gather the relevant factual information.
    b. Analyze the facts to determine the most appropriate moral values.
    c. Make an ethical judgment based on the rightness or wrongness of the proposed activity or policy.
    d. Make an ethical judgment based on what the CEO thinks is right.

3. Which of the following is NOT one of the four fundamental ethical norms?
    a. Self-interest   b. Utility
    c. Justice   d. Caring

4. Written codes of ethical conduct established by businesses are designed to do all of the following EXCEPT
    a. increase public confidence in a firm or its industry.
    b. increase government regulation.
    c. improve internal operations by providing consistent standards of both ethical and legal conduct.
    d. help managers respond to problems that arise as a result of unethical or illegal behavior.

5. Which of the following is a stakeholder group to which business has a responsibility?
    a. Consumers and society in general   b. Investors
    c. Employees   d. All of the above.

6. One of the most common approaches to formalizing top management commitment to ethical business practices is
    a. abandoning ethics programs already in place.
    b. telling individual employees about new policies verbally.
    c. adopting written codes.
    d. None of the above.

7.   Which of the following statements is *true*?
      a. One way companies can evaluate their ethical standards is by conducting a
          social audit.
      b. The only real stakeholders to a company are investors.
      c. The idea that business has certain obligations to society beyond the pursuit of
          profits faded in the 1980s.
      d. Rarely do businesses profit from socially responsible behavior.

8.   Which of the following statements is *false*?
      a. Socially responsible business behavior is a concept that dates back to at least the
          late 1800s.
      b. Government laws and regulations designed to prevent pollution have, in
          practice, only made pollution worse.
      c. Sometimes, costs of production, and therefore prices, are higher when
          businesses take the steps necessary to pollute less.
      d. The three major kinds of pollution are air, water, and land pollution.

9.   Consumerism
      a. began in the 1960s.
      b. is a movement that pressures businesses to consider consumer needs
          and interests.
      c. prompted many businesses to create consumer affairs departments.
      d. All of the above.

10.   Which of the following is NOT included as one of President John F. Kennedy's
      "bill of rights" for consumers?
      a. The right to a fair price
      b. The right to be informed about all relevant aspects of a product
      c. The right to safe products
      d. The right to choose what one buys

11.   Government product labeling requirements, for example on canned goods,
      demonstrate a response to which of the following consumer rights?
      a. The right to be heard
      b. The right to be informed about all relevant aspects of a product
      c. The right to choose what one buys
      d. The right to complain

12.   Investors
      a. can be cheated if they are not provided the expected rate of return on
          their funds.
      b. are very rarely cheated.
      c. can be cheated if companies or individuals misrepresent the value of an
          investment, or if company funds are diverted by managers for their
          personal use.
      d. All of the above.

13. Questionable business practices include
     a. insider trading.
     b. paying excessive salaries to senior managers.
     c. not conforming to generally accepted accounting practices.
     d. All of the above.

14. A company that has little regard for ethical conduct and will generally go to great
     lengths to hide wrongdoing would be practicing the
     a. obstructionist stance to social responsibility.
     b. defensive stance to social responsibility.
     c. accommodative stance to social responsibility.
     d. proactive stance to social responsibility.

15. The highest degree of social responsibility that a firm can exhibit is the
     a. obstructionist stance.   b. accommodative stance.
     b. defensive stance.   d. proactive stance.

Match the Terms and Concepts with Their Definitions

a. ethics   f. organizational stakeholders   k. obstructionist stance
b. ethical behavior   g. consumerism   l. defensive stance
c. unethical behavior   h. collusion   m. accommodative stance
d. business ethics   i. whistle-blower   n. proactive stance
e. social responsibility   j. managerial ethics   o. greenwashing

_____ 1. Behavior that does not conform to generally accepted social norms concerning
           beneficial and harmful actions.

_____ 2. An approach to social responsibility by which a company, if specifically asked
           to do so, exceeds legal minimums in its commitments to groups and
           individuals in its social environment.

_____ 3. An employee who detects and tries to put an end to a company's unethical,
           illegal, or socially irresponsible actions by publicizing them.

_____ 4. The attempt of a business to balance its commitments to groups and
           individuals in its environment, including customers, other businesses,
           employees, and investors.

_____ 5. An approach to social responsibility that involves doing as little as possible
           and may involve attempts to deny or cover up violations.

_____ 6. A form of social activism dedicated to protecting the rights of consumers in
           their dealings with businesses.

_____ 7. Beliefs about what is right and wrong or good and bad in actions that affect others.

_____ 8. Using advertising to project a green image without adopting substantive environmentally friendly changes.

_____ 9. Ethical or unethical behaviors by a manager or employer of an organization.

_____ 10. An illegal agreement between two or more companies to commit a wrongful act.

_____ 11. An approach to social responsibility by which a company meets only minimum legal requirements in its commitments to groups and individuals in its social environment.

_____ 12. Those groups, individuals, and organizations that are directly affected by the practices of an organization and who therefore have a stake in its performance.

_____ 13. Standards of behavior that guide individual managers in their work.

_____ 14. Behavior conforming to generally accepted social norms concerning beneficial and harmful actions.

_____ 15. An approach to social responsibility by which a company actively seeks opportunities to contribute to the well being of groups and individuals in its social environment.

Fill in the Blanks

1. Groups and individuals who are directly affected by the practices of an organization and have a stake in its performance are _____.

2. A _____ is an employee who discovers and tries to put an end to a company's unethical, illegal, or socially irresponsible actions by publicizing them.

3. _____ is using confidential information to gain from the purchase or sale of stocks.

4. _____ are systematic analyses of an organization's success in using funds earmarked for its social responsibility goals.

5. _____ are the standards of behavior that guide individual managers in their work.

Learning Objectives—Short Answer or Essay Questions

Learning Objective #1: Explain how individuals develop their personal codes of ethics and why ethics are important in the workplace.

Learning Objective #2: Distinguish social responsibility from ethics, identify organizational stakeholders, and trace the evolution of social responsibility in U.S. business.

Learning Objective #3: Show how the concept of social responsibility applies both to environmental issues and to a firm's relationships with its customers, employees, and investors.

Learning Objective #4: Identify four general approaches to social responsibility and describe the four steps a firm must take to implement a social responsibility program.

Learning Objective #5: Explain how issues of social responsibility and ethics affect small business.

Critical Thinking Questions

1. Discuss what is necessary for a social responsibility program to be successful.

2. What does a company risk when it does not act responsibly toward its customers?

3. Describe how you might recognize a situation where a conflict of interest might occur.

Brain Teaser

What can business organizations do to improve the ethical behavior of their employees?

ANSWERS

True-False—Answers

1. True
2. False: Global variations can complicate ethical business practices.
3. False: Using advertising to project a green image without adopting substantive environmentally friendly changes is greenwashing.
4. True
5. True
6. True
7. True
8. False: Insider trading is using confidential information to gain from the purchase or sale of stocks.
9. False: Firms with the highest degree of social responsibility exhibit the proactive stance.
10. False: The first step in assessing ethical behavior is to gather the relevant factual information.
11. False: The lowest level of social responsibility is the obstructionist stance.
12. False: Managerial ethics are the standards of behavior that guide individual managers in their work.
13. False: Consumerism is a form of social activism dedicated to protecting the rights of consumers in their dealings with businesses.
14. True
15. True
16. True
17. True
18. True
19. False: A conflict of interest occurs when an activity may benefit the individual to the detriment of his or her employer.
20. True

Multiple Choice—Answers

1. d	4. b	7. a	10. a	13. d
2. d	5. d	8. b	11. b	14. a
3. a	6. c	9. d	12. c	15. d

Match the Terms and Concepts with Their Definitions—Answers

1. c	4. e	7. a	10. h	13. j
2. m	5. k	8. o	11. l	14. b
3. i	6. g	9. d	12. f	15. n

Fill in the Blanks—Answers

1. organizational stakeholders
2. whistle-blower
3. insider trading
4. social audits
5. managerial ethics

Learning Objectives—Short Answer or Essay Questions—Answers

Learning Objective #1: Explain how individuals develop their personal codes of ethics and why ethics are important in the workplace.
Individual *codes of ethics* are derived from social standards of right and wrong. *Ethical behavior* is behavior that conforms to generally accepted social norms concerning beneficial and harmful actions. Because ethics affect the behavior of individuals on behalf of the companies that employ them, many firms are adopting formal statements of ethics. Unethical behavior can result in loss of business, fines, and even imprisonment.

Learning Objective #2: Distinguish social responsibility from ethics, identify organizational stakeholders, and trace the evolution of social responsibility in U.S. business.
Social responsibility refers to an organization's response to social needs. One way to understand social responsibility is to view it in terms of *stakeholders*—those groups, individuals, and organizations that are directly affected by the practices of an organization and that therefore have a stake in its performance. Until the second half of the nineteenth century, businesses often paid little attention to stakeholders. Since then, however, both public pressure and government regulation, especially as a result of the Great Depression of the 1930s and the social activism of the 1960s and 1970s, have forced businesses to consider the public welfare, at least to some degree. A trend toward increased social consciousness, including a heightened sense of environmental activism, has recently emerged.

Learning Objective #3: Show how the concept of social responsibility applies both to environmental issues and to a firm's relationships with its customers, employees, and investors.
Social responsibility toward the environment requires firms to minimize pollution of air, water, and land. Social responsibility toward customers requires firms to provide products of acceptable quality, to price products fairly, and to respect consumers' rights. Social responsibility toward employees requires firms to respect workers both as resources and as people who are more productive when their needs are met. Social responsibility toward investors requires firms to manage resources and to represent their financial status honestly.

Learning Objective #4: Identify four general approaches to social responsibility and describe the four steps a firm must take to implement a social responsibility program.
An *obstructionist stance* on social responsibility is taken by a firm that does as little as possible to address social or environmental problems and that may deny or attempt to cover up problems that may occur. The *defensive stance* emphasizes compliance with legal minimum requirements. Companies adopting the *accommodative stance* go beyond minimum activities, if asked. The *proactive stance* commits a company to actively seek to contribute to social projects. Implementing a social responsibility program entails four steps: (1) drafting a policy statement with the support of top management, (2) developing a detailed plan, (3) appointing a director to implement the plan, and (4) conducting *social audits* to monitor results.

Learning Objective #5: Explain how issues of social responsibility and ethics affect small business.
Managers and employees of small businesses face many of the same ethical questions as their counterparts at larger firms. Small businesses face the same issues of social responsibility and the same need to decide on an approach to social responsibility. The differences are primarily differences of scale.

Critical Thinking Questions—Answers

1. **Discuss what is necessary for a social responsibility program to be successful.**
   Social responsibility must start at the top and be considered a factor in strategic planning. No program can succeed without the support of top management, who must embrace a strong stand on social responsibility and develop a policy statement outlining that commitment.

2. **What does a company risk when it does not act responsibly towards its customers?**
   A company that does not act responsibly toward its customers will ultimately lose their trust and their business. To encourage responsibility, the FTC regulates advertising and pricing practices, and the FDA enforces labeling guidelines for food products. These government regulating bodies can impose penalties against violators, who may also face civil litigation.

3. **Describe how you might recognize a situation where a conflict of interest might occur.**

   A conflict of interest occurs when an activity may benefit the individual to the detriment of his or her employer. To avoid even the appearance of bribery or favoritism, most companies have policies that forbid buyers from accepting gifts from suppliers. Relatively common problems in the general area of honesty include stealing supplies and padding expense accounts.

Brain Teaser—Answer

What can business organizations do to improve the ethical behavior of their employees?

To discourage unethical and illegal activities, companies have taken formal steps, such as setting up codes of conduct; developing clear ethical positions; and perhaps most effectively, demonstrating upper-management support of ethical standards. These policies contribute to a corporate culture that values ethical standards and announce that the firm is equally concerned with good citizenship and profits.

Chapter 3
Entrepreneurship, New Ventures, and Business Ownership

Learning Objectives
After reading this chapter, you should be able to:

1. Define *small business*, discuss its importance to the U.S. economy, and explain popular areas of small business.
2. Explain entrepreneurship and describe some key characteristics of entrepreneurial personalities and activities.
3. Describe the business plan and the start-up decisions made by small businesses and identify sources of financial aid available to such enterprises.
4. Discuss the trends in small business start-ups and identify the main reasons for success and failure among small businesses.
5. Explain sole proprietorships, partnerships, and cooperatives, and discuss advantages and disadvantages of each.
6. Describe corporations, discuss their advantages and disadvantages, and identify different kinds of corporations.
7. Explain the basic issues involved in managing a corporation and discuss special issues related to corporate ownership.

True-False
Indicate whether the statement is generally true or false by placing a "T" or an "F" in the space provided. If it is a false statement, correct it so that it becomes a true statement.

_____ 1. Although the term *small business* defies easy definition, a small business can be considered an independently owned and managed business that does not dominate its market.

_____ 2. The Small Business Administration (SBA) is a government agency that serves as a resource and advocate for small firms.

_____ 3. Small companies tend to be innovative, partly because company owners are more accessible and partly because these companies offer more opportunity for individual expression.

_____ 4. Running a small business takes a lot of hard work, drive, and dedication, and being a successful corporate employee doesn't necessarily translate into being a successful small-business owner.

_____ 5. Small businesses do not provide very many new jobs.

_____ 6. Service businesses are the fastest growing segment of the small-business enterprise.

_____ 7. Small businesses have accounted for a small fraction of the nation's new product developments.

_____ 8. In general, entrepreneurs want to remain small and simply support a lifestyle with their businesses, whereas small-business owners are motivated to grow and expand their businesses.

_____ 9. Female entrepreneurs make up one of the fastest-growing segments in the small-business economy.

_____ 10. You can start a new business from scratch by buying an existing business or investing in a franchise.

_____ 11. Beyond personal funds, two other sources of start-up funds are venture capital companies and small-business investment companies.

_____ 12. Hoping to boost their economies and create jobs, state and local governments have launched many programs to help small businesses.

_____ 13. SBA loans are a major source of small-business financing.

_____ 14. Management advice from advisory boards, management consultants, the SBA, and networking is usually not available to small-business owners.

_____ 15. A *franchisee* is the seller of a franchise, whereas a *franchiser* is the buyer of the franchise.

_____ 16. One disadvantage of a franchise is wide name recognition and mass advertising of the good or service sold.

_____ 17. One advantage of a franchise is the managerial support provided by the franchiser.

_____ 18. One disadvantage of a franchise is the possible continued obligation to contribute percentages of sales revenues to parent corporations.

_____ 19. Sole proprietorships are always small.

_____ 20. A major advantage of sole proprietorships is unlimited liability.

_____ 21. General partnerships are the most popular form of business.

Multiple Choice

Circle the best answer for each of the following questions.

1. Which of the following statements is *true*?
    a. Small businesses are a very important part of the U.S. economy.
    b. Unlike entrepreneurs, small-business owners intend to grow their businesses very rapidly to earn very large profits.
    c. Very few of the products made by big manufacturers are sold to consumers by small businesses.
    d. All of the above.

2. Small businesses are characterized by
    a. being innovative.
    b. having relatively little influence in their markets.
    c. their owners working hard to perform a variety of job functions.
    d. All of the above.

3. Which of the following is *false* about small businesses in our economy?
    a. Small businesses provide jobs for a significant part of the labor force.
    b. Small businesses rarely sell services.
    c. Small businesses supply many of the needs of large corporations.
    d. Small businesses provide for many new innovations and product developments.

4. In which of the following sectors of our economy are small businesses least likely to be found?
    a. Services
    b. Retailing
    c. Finance and insurance
    d. Manufacturing

5. Which of the following is *true* about entrepreneurs?
    a. An entrepreneur is any small-business owner.
    b. Entrepreneurs assume the risk of business ownership with a primary goal of growth and expansion.
    c. Entrepreneurs are rarely concerned about good personal customer relations.
    d. Entrepreneurs avoid risk whenever possible.

6. Factors that account for the rapid start-up of new small businesses include
    a. the emergence of e-commerce.
    b. increased opportunities for minorities and women.
    c. new opportunities in global enterprise.
    d. All of the above.

7. Which of the following is NOT one of the reasons for small business failure?
   a. Managerial incompetence or inexperience
   b. Effective control systems
   c. Insufficient capital
   d. Neglect

8. Small business success can be attributed to
   a. luck.
   b. hard work, drive, and dedication.
   c. a high demand for the good or service produced.
   d. All of the above.

9. A way to get into business for yourself is to
   a. start a new company from scratch.
   b. buy an existing business.
   c. invest in a franchise.
   d. All of the above.

10. When starting a small business
    a. the first step is the individual's commitment to becoming a business owner.
    b. one needs to select the good or service to be offered for sale.
    c. one must understand the true nature of the enterprise.
    d. All of the above.

11. Which of the following statements is *true*?
    a. If you apply to several banks for financing and are turned down by all of them, you may be able to qualify for a loan backed by the SBA.
    b. Venture capital companies are federally licensed to borrow money from the SBA and to invest it in or lend it to small businesses.
    c. Small-business investment companies are groups of small investors seeking to make profits on companies with rapid growth potential.
    d. All of the above.

12. When small businesses are loaned funds put up jointly by banks and the SBA, this is
    a. a guaranteed loans program.
    b. an immediate participation loans program.
    c. a local development companies program.
    d. a venture capital loans program.

13. An SBA program in which retired executives work with small businesses on a volunteer basis is the
    a. Active Corps of Executives (ACE).
    b. Small Business Institute (SBI).
    c. Service Corps of Retired Executives (SCORE).
    d. Small Business Development Center (SBDC).

14. Which of the following is *true*?
    a. In a strategic alliance, two or more organizations collaborate on a project for mutual gain.
    b. SCORE is a resource for small-business management advice.
    c. Small Business Development Centers consolidate information from various disciplines and institutions and make this knowledge available to new and existing small businesses.
    d. All of the above.

15. Which of the following statements is *false*?
    a. Franchising is very common.
    b. A franchise enables one to use a larger company's trade name and sell its products or services in a specific territory.
    c. A franchisee never has to pay the franchiser a percentage of sales revenues.
    d. A franchise may constrain the franchisee's independence.

16. Which of the following statements is *false*?
    a. Owning a franchise rarely involves any considerable start-up expense.
    b. A franchisee has the advantage of training and managerial support from the franchiser.
    c. A franchisee may have the advantage of financial support from the franchiser.
    d. A franchisee has the advantage of wide name recognition and mass advertising provided by the franchiser.

17. Which of the following is *false*?
    a. If an entrepreneur is good at launching a business, then he or she is assured of success in managing the business over the long term.
    b. One way companies expand their business is by franchising their concepts to others.
    c. The starting point for virtually every new business is a business plan.
    d. By using the Internet, smaller firms can compete with bigger firms.

18. Which of the following is *false*?
    a. One reason for the failure of small businesses is lack of managerial experience.
    b. One reason for the failure of small businesses is that most entrepreneurs are younger than 25 years old.
    c. One reason for the failure of small businesses is neglect.
    d. One reason for the failure of small businesses is weak control systems.

19. Which of the following is NOT an advantage of partnerships?
    a. The ability to grow by adding new talent
    b. The relative ease of formation
    c. Unlimited liability
    d. Lenders are more apt to lend money to partnerships than sole proprietorships

20. In which of the following do two or more organizations collaborate on a project for
    mutual gain?
    a. Limited partnership
    b. Public corporation
    c. Strategic alliance
    d. Joint venture

Match the Terms and Concepts with Their Definitions

a. Small Business Administration   g. guaranteed loans program   m. sole proprietorship
b. small business   h. limited partner   n. Small Business
                                                                           Dev. Center
                                                                           (SBDC)
c. entrepreneur   i. certified development   o. unlimited liability
                                         company (504) program
d. venture capital company   j. stock   p. franchise
e. small-business investment   k. Service Corps of Retired
   company (SBIC)   Executives (SCORE)
f. minority enterprise small-   l. publicly held (or public)
business investment company   corporation
(MESBIC)

_____ 1. A businessperson who accepts both the risks and the opportunities involved in
            creating and operating a new business.

_____ 2. A business owned and operated by one person who is responsible for all of
            its debts.

_____ 3. Legal principle holding owners responsible for paying off all debts of
            a business.

_____ 4. A federally sponsored company that specializes in financing businesses that
            are owned and operated by minorities.

_____ 5. A program in which the SBA works with nonprofit community-based lenders
            to boost a community's economy.

_____ 6. An independently owned and managed business that has relatively little
            influence in its market.

_____ 7. An arrangement in which a buyer (franchisee) purchases the right to sell the
            good or service of the seller (franchiser).

_____ 8. A corporation whose stock is widely held and available for sale to the general public.

_____ 9. A government-regulated investment company that borrows money from the SBA to invest in or lend to a small business.

_____ 10. A partner who does not share in a firm's management and is liable for its debts only to the limits of said partner's investment.

_____ 11. A group of small investors who invest money in companies with rapid growth potential.

_____ 12. An SBA program designed to consolidate information from various disciplines and make it available to small businesses.

_____ 13. An SBA program in which retired executives work with small businesses voluntarily.

_____ 14. A federal agency charged with assisting small businesses.

_____ 15. A program in which the SBA guarantees to repay 75 to 85 percent of small-business commercial loans up to $750,000.

_____ 16. A share of ownership in a corporation.

Let's List

Answer the following questions with a series of lists:

1. Identify the common characteristics successful entrepreneurs share.

   a. _____
   b. _____
   c. _____
   d. _____

2. List the three specific questions that must be answered in a business plan.

   a. _____
   b. _____
   c. _____

3. List four major factors that contribute to failures of new businesses.

    a. _____

    b. _____

    c. _____

    d. _____

4. List four major SBA financial programs.

    a. _____

    b. _____

    c. _____

    d. _____

Learning Objectives—Short Answer or Essay Questions

Learning Objective #1: Define *small business*, discuss its importance to the U.S. economy, and explain popular areas of small business.

Learning Objective #2: Explain entrepreneurship and describe some key characteristics of entrepreneurial personalities and activities.

Learning Objective #3: Describe the business plan and the start-up decisions made by small businesses and identify sources of financial aid available to such enterprises.

Learning Objective #4: Discuss the trends in small business start-ups and identify the main reasons for success and failure among small businesses.

Learning Objective #5: Explain sole proprietorships, partnerships, and cooperatives, and discuss the advantages and disadvantages of each.

Learning Objective #6: Describe corporations, discuss their advantages and disadvantages, and identify different kinds of corporations.

Learning Objective #7: Explain the basic issues involved in managing a corporation and discuss special issues related to corporate ownership.

Critical Thinking Questions

1. What is the biggest advantage of incorporating a small business?

2. What motivates an entrepreneur to start a new business?

Brain Teaser

Why would small-business owners consider joining or forming a cooperative?

ANSWERS

True-False—Answers

1.   True
2.   True
3.   True
4.   True
5.   False: Small businesses *are a principle source of* new jobs.
6.   True
7.   False: Small businesses have accounted for a *large* fraction of the nation's new product developments.
8.   False: *Small-business owners* want to remain small and simply support a lifestyle; *entrepreneurs* are motivated to grow and to expand their businesses.
9.   True
10. True
11. True
12. True
13. False: SBA loans are *not* a major source of small-business financing.
14. False: Management advice from advisory boards, management consultants, the SBA, and networking *is usually readily available* to small-business owners.
15. False: A franchisee is the *buyer* of a franchise, whereas a franchiser is the *seller* of the franchise.
16. False: One *advantage* of a franchise is wide name recognition and mass advertising of the good or service sold.
17. True
18. True
19. False: Sole proprietorships are *not* always small.
20. False: A major *disadvantage* of sole proprietorships is unlimited liability.
21. False: General partnerships are the *least* popular form of business.

Multiple Choice—Answers

1. a	5. b	9. d	13. c	17. a
2. d	6. d	10. d	14. d	18. b
3. b	7. b	11. a	15. c	19. c
4. d	8. d	12. b	16. a	20. c

Match the Terms and Concepts with Their Definitions—Answers

1. c	5. i	9. e	13. k
2. m	6. b	10. h	14. a
3. o	7. p	11. d	15. g
4. f	8. l	12. n	16. j

Let's List—Answers

1. Identify the common characteristics successful entrepreneurs share.
    a. Resourcefulness
    b. Concern for good customer relations
    c. Ability to deal with uncertainty and risk
    d. Desire to be their own bosses

2. List the three specific questions that must be answered in a business plan.
    a. What are the entrepreneur's goals and objectives?
    b. What strategies will be used to obtain them?
    c. How will these strategies be implemented?

3. List four major factors that contribute to failures of new businesses.
    a. Managerial incompetence or inexperience
    b. Neglect
    c. Weak control systems
    d. Insufficient capital

4. List four major SBA financial programs.
    a. 7(a) loan program
    b. Special purpose loans
    c. Micro-loan program
    d. Certified development company (504) program

Learning Objectives—Short Answer or Essay Questions—Answers

Learning Objective #1: Define *small business*, discuss its importance to the U.S. economy, and explain popular areas of small business.
A *small business* is independently owned and managed and does not dominate its market. Small businesses are crucial to the economy because they create new jobs, foster entrepreneurship and innovation, and supply goods and services needed by larger businesses. Services are the easiest operations for small-business owners to start because they require low levels of resources. They also offer high returns on investment and tend to foster innovation. Retailing and wholesaling are more difficult because they usually require some experience, but they are still attractive to many entrepreneurs. Construction, financial, and insurance operations are also common sectors for small business. As the most resource-intensive areas of the economy, transportation and manufacturing are the areas least populated by small firms.

Learning Objective #2: Explain entrepreneurship and describe some key characteristics of entrepreneurial personalities and activities.

Entrepreneurship is the process of seeking business opportunities under conditions of risk. Entrepreneurs are people who assume the risk of business ownership. Some entrepreneurs have a goal of independence and financial security, while others want to launch a new venture that can be grown into a large business. Most successful entrepreneurs are resourceful and concerned for customer relations. They have a strong desire to be their own boss and can handle ambiguity and surprises. Today's entrepreneur is often an open-minded leader who relies on networks, business plans, and consensus, and is just as likely to be female as male. Finally, although successful entrepreneurs understand the role of risk, they do not necessarily regard what they do as being risky.

Learning Objective #3: Describe the business plan and the start-up decisions made by small businesses and identify sources of financial aid available to such enterprises.

A *business plan* is the starting point for virtually every new business. In it, the entrepreneur summarizes business strategy for the new venture and shows how it will be implemented. Business plans are increasingly important because creditors and investors demand them as tools for deciding whether to finance or invest. Entrepreneurs must also decide whether to buy an existing business, operate a franchise, or start from scratch.

Common funding sources include personal funds, family and friends, savings, lenders, investors, and governmental agencies. Venture capital companies are groups of small investors seeking to make profits on companies with rapid growth potential. Most of these firms do not lend money but rather invest it, supplying capital in return for partial ownership. Lending institutions are more likely to finance an existing business than a new business because the risks are better understood.

Learning Objective #4: Discuss the trends in small business start-ups and identify the main reasons for success and failure among small businesses.

Five factors account for the fact that thousands of new businesses are started in the United States every year: (1) the emergence of e-commerce, (2) entrepreneurs who cross over from big business, (3) increased opportunities for minorities and women, (4) new opportunities in global enterprise, and (5) improved rates of survival among small businesses.

Four factors contribute to most small-business failure: (1) managerial incompetence or inexperience, (2) neglect, (3) weak control systems, and (4) insufficient capital. Likewise, four basic factors explain most small-business success: (1) hard work, drive, and dedication; (2) market demand for the products or services being provided; (3) managerial competence; and (4) luck.

Learning Objective #5: Explain sole proprietorships, partnerships, and cooperatives, and discuss the advantages and disadvantages of each.
The *sole proprietorship* is owned and usually operated by one person. There are tax benefits for new businesses that are likely to suffer losses in early stages. A major drawback is *unlimited liability.* Another disadvantage is lack of continuity. Finally, a sole proprietorship depends on the resources of a single individual. The *general partnership* is a sole proprietorship multiplied by the number of partner-owners. The biggest advantage is its ability to grow by adding new talent and money. A partnership is not a legal entity; it is just two or more people working together. Partners are taxed as individuals, and *unlimited liability* is a drawback. Partnerships may lack continuity, and transferring ownership may be hard. No partner may sell out without the consent of the others. *Cooperatives* combine the freedom of sole proprietorships with the financial power of corporations.

Learning Objective #6: Describe corporations, discuss their advantages and disadvantages, and identify different kinds of corporations.
All corporations share certain characteristics: legal status as separate entities, property rights and obligations, and indefinite life spans. They may sue and be sued; buy, hold, and sell property; make and sell products; and commit crimes and be tried and punished for them. The biggest advantage of incorporation is *limited liability*: investor liability is limited to one's personal investments in the corporation. Another advantage is continuity. Finally, corporations have advantages in raising money. By selling stock, they expand the number of investors and the amount of available funds. Legal protections tend to make lenders more willing to grant loans.

One disadvantage is that a corporation can be taken over against the will of its managers. Another disadvantage is start-up cost. Corporations are heavily regulated and must meet complex legal requirements in the states in which they're chartered. The greatest potential drawback to incorporation is double taxation. Different kinds of corporations help businesses take advantage of incorporation without assuming all of the disadvantages.

Learning Objective #7: Explain the basic issues involved in managing a corporation and discuss special issues related to corporate ownership.
Creating a corporation, regardless of its type, can be complicated. In addition, once the corporate entity has come into existence, it must be managed by people who understand the complex principles of *corporate governance*—the roles of shareholders, directors, and other managers in corporate decision making. It is important to understand the principles of *stock ownership* and *stockholders' rights* and the role of the *boards of directors.* In recent years, several special issues have arisen or grown in importance in corporate ownership. The most important of these trends are *joint ventures* and *strategic alliances, employee stock ownership plans*, and *institutional ownership.* Other important issues in contemporary corporate ownership involve *mergers, acquisitions, divestitures,* and *spin-offs.*

Critical Thinking Questions—Answers

1. **What is the biggest advantage of incorporating a small business?**
   The biggest advantage of corporations is limited liability: investor liability is limited to personal investment in the corporation.

2. **What motivates an entrepreneur to start a new business?**
   Many entrepreneurs are driven to launch new businesses by the goal of gaining independence from working for someone else and securing a financial future for themselves, but they may not aspire to grow their businesses beyond their capacities to run them.

Brain Teaser—Answer

Why would small-business owners consider joining or forming a cooperative?

Groups of sole proprietorships or partnerships may agree to work together for their common benefit by forming cooperatives, which combine the freedom of sole proprietorships with the financial power of corporations.

Chapter 4
The Global Context of Business

ter reading this chapter, you should be able to:

Discuss the rise of international business and describe the major world marketplaces and trade agreements and alliances.

Explain how differences in import-export balances, exchange rates, and foreign competition determine the ways in which countries and businesses respond to the international environment.

Discuss the factors involved in deciding to do business internationally and in selecting the appropriate levels of international involvement and international organizational structure.

Describe some of the ways in which social, cultural, economic, legal, and political differences among nations affect international business.

rue-False
dicate whether the statement is generally true or false by placing a "T" or an "F" in the space ovided. If it is a false statement, correct it so that it becomes a true statement.

____ 1. The contemporary world economy revolves around three major marketplaces: North America, Europe, and Africa.

____ 2. Canada is the United States' largest trading partner.

____ 3. If a nation has a comparative advantage in the production of a good, it means that the nation is relatively more efficient at producing that good than any other nation.

____ 4. The balance of payments refers to the amount of goods a nation imports and exports; balance of trade refers to the amount of money flowing in and out of the country.

____ 5. A strong dollar would increase exports from the United States and reduce its imports, creating a trade surplus.

____ 6. The business climate in other nations is one key factor for a business considering international expansion.

____ 7. After a firm decides to expand internationally, it must decide whether to be an exporter or importer, to organize as an international firm, or to operate as a multinational firm.

_____ 8. A licensing arrangement is a cooperative partnership in which firms choose foreign individuals to manufacture or market their products in another country.

_____ 9. A strategic alliance is an arrangement in which a company finds a foreign partner to contribute approximately half of the resources needed to establish and operate a new business in the partner's country.

_____ 10. Importing is the investment of money by foreign companies in domestic business enterprises.

_____ 11. Cultural differences are not very important when conducting international business.

_____ 12. An international business needs to learn as much as possible about the culture of the foreign countries it does business with.

_____ 13. A subsidy is a government payment to help a domestic business compete with foreign firms.

_____ 14. A quota is a tax on an imported product; a tariff is a limit on the quantity allowed to enter the country.

_____ 15. Supporters of protectionism argue that tariffs and quotas protect domestic firms and jobs as well as shelter new industries until they're able to compete internationally.

_____ 16. Business practice laws can differ significantly among nations.

_____ 17. The Organization of Petroleum Exporting Countries (OPEC) is considered a cartel.

Multiple Choice
Circle the best answer for each of the following questions.

1. Globalization has accelerated due to
    a. governments and businesses becoming more aware of the benefits of globalization to their countries and shareholders.
    b. new technologies that have made international travel, communication, and commerce easier, faster, and cheaper.
    c. competitive pressures forcing firms to enter foreign markets just to keep pace with competitors.
    d. All of the above.

2. Which of the following statements is *false?*
   a. According to the World Bank, a low-income country has a per capita income of less than $9,386, but more than $765.
   b. Even if a nation does not have an absolute advantage, it is still beneficial for that nation to participate in international trade if it has a comparative advantage.
   c. Nations trade with each other because they are better off by doing so.
   d. Globalization is becoming increasingly more prevalent.

3. One of the conditions for a country to experience a national competitive advantage in the production of a product is
   a. an inadequate quantity of natural resources to produce that product.
   b. the presence of consumers who are not particular about quality or innovation.
   c. strong local or regional suppliers and/or industrial customers.
   d. the presence of firms and industries that do not stress cost reduction, product quality, and higher productivity, and are not particularly innovative.

4. An increase in the value of the U.S. dollar (a "stronger" dollar) would
   a. reduce the relative price of American-made goods for foreigners.
   b. increase the relative price of foreign-made goods for Americans.
   c. increase U.S. imports.
   d. create a trade surplus for the United States.

5. Which of the following is *true*?
   a. An *importer* is a firm that makes products in one country and then distributes and sells them in others.
   b. An *international firm* conducts a significant portion of its business abroad.
   c. A *multinational firm* is a very large corporation that has been successful in out-competing foreign firms in its home market but does not compete in foreign markets.
   d. All of the above.

6. Licensing is
   a. purchasing goods or services from another country and bringing them into one's own country.
   b. an agreement to produce and market another company's product in exchange for a royalty or fee.
   c. an arrangement in which a company finds a foreign partner to contribute approximately half of the resources needed to establish and operate a new business in the partner's country.
   d. sending some managers from the home office to run overseas operations.

7. Investment of money by foreign companies in domestic business enterprises is
   a. exporting.
   b. licensing.
   c. foreign direct investment (FDI).
   d. a subsidy.

8. To improve international competitiveness, firms need to
    a. learn as much as possible about the cultures of the countries they work with.
    b. keep an open mind, avoid stereotyping, and learn how to show respect in another culture.
    c. learn as much as possible about the economic, legal, and political differences among nations.
    d. All of the above.

9. Which of the following statements is true?
    a. Protectionism typically increases employment for a nation as a whole over time.
    b. Dumping is charging less for a product abroad than the actual cost of production.
    c. A quota is a tax on an imported good, while a tariff is a limit on the quantity allowed to enter the country.
    d. Rarely are trade barriers politically popular.

10. Which of the following is *not* a trade barrier (a form of protectionism)?
    a. Local content requirements   b. Embargoes
    c. Foreign direct investment (FDI)   d. Subsidies

11. Which of the following is *not* an argument in favor of protectionism?
    a. Protectionism preserves domestic jobs.
    b. Protectionism helps weak domestic industries stay afloat.
    c. Protectionism allows a nation to retaliate against unfair foreign competition.
    d. None of the above.

12. The set of requirements that states that products sold in a country be at least partly made there is called
    a. local content laws.   b. business practice laws.
    c. embargo rights laws.   d. consumer safety laws.

Match the Terms and Concepts with Their Definitions

a. globalization
b. per capita income
c. import
d. export
e. absolute advantage
f. comparative advantage
g. national competitive advantage
h. balance of trade
i. trade deficit
j. trade surplus
k. balance of payments

l. exchange rate
m. Euro
n. exporter
o. importer
p. international firm
q. multinational firm
r. independent agent

s. licensing arrangement
t. royalty
u. strategic alliance

v. foreign direct investment
w. quota
x. embargo
y. tariff
z. subsidy
aa. protectionism
bb. local content law

cc. business practice laws
dd. cartel
ee. dumping

_____ 1.   A product made or grown domestically but shipped and sold abroad.

_____ 2.   A firm that buys products in foreign markets and then imports them for resale in its home country.

_____ 3.   An arrangement in which a firm buys or establishes assets in another country.

_____ 4.   The economic value of all products a country exports minus the economic value of all products it imports.

_____ 5.   The ability to produce some products more efficiently than others.

_____ 6.   The practice of selling a product abroad for less than the cost of production.

_____ 7.   A firm that designs, produces, and markets products in many nations.

_____ 8.   International competitive advantage stemming from a combination of factor conditions, demand conditions, related and supporting industries, and firm strategies, structures, and rivalries.

_____ 9.   The average income per person in a country.

_____ 10. An arrangement in which a company finds a foreign partner to contribute approximately half of the resources needed to establish and operate a new business in the partner's country.

_____ 11. The flow of all money into or out of a country.

_____ 12. The laws or regulations governing business practices in given countries.

_____ 13. The government order banning exportation and/or importation of a particular product or all products from a particular country.

_____ 14. A situation in which a country's imports exceed its exports, creating a negative balance of trade.

_____ 15. A firm that distributes and sells products to one or more foreign countries.

_____ 16. The process by which the world economy is becoming an interdependent system.

_____ 17. Payment made to a license holder in return for the right to market the licenser's product.

_____ 18. The law requiring that products sold in a particular country be at least partly made there.

_____ 19. A foreign individual or organization that agrees to represent an exporter's interests.

_____ 20. A situation in which a country's exports exceed its imports

_____ 21. A product made or grown abroad but sold domestically.

_____ 22. The restriction on the number of products of a certain type that can be imported to a country.

_____ 23. The practice of protecting domestic business against foreign competition.

_____ 24. The rate at which currency of one nation can be exchanged for currency of another country.

_____ 25. Tax levied on imported products.

_____ 26. The ability to produce something more efficiently than any other country can.

_____ 27. An association of producers whose purpose is to control supply and prices.

_____ 28. Common currency created by the European Union.

_____ 29. An arrangement in which firms choose foreign individuals or organizations to manufacture or market their products in another country.

_____ 30. A firm that conducts a significant portion of its business in foreign countries.

_____ 31. Government payment to help a domestic business compete with foreign firms.

Jeopardy

Complete the question to each of the following answers as quickly as you can.

International Business	Import-Export Balances	International Organizational Structures
Process of the world economy fast becoming an interdependent system What is _____?	When a country's imports exceeds its exports What is a/n _____?	Foreign individual that represents an exporter What is a/n_____?
Products made or grown abroad and sold domestically in the U.S. What are _____?	The flow of money into or out of a country What is a/n _____?	When a company finds a partner in the country in which it does business What is a/n _____?
Products made or grown here and shipped for sale abroad What are _____?	The rate at which the currency of one nation is exchanged for that of another What is the _____?	When firms give foreign individuals exclusive rights to manufacture a product What is a/n _____?

Learning Objectives—Short Answer or Essay Questions

Learning Objective #1: Discuss the rise of international business and describe the major world marketplaces and trade agreements and alliances.

Learning Objective #2: Explain how differences in import-export balances, exchange rates, and foreign competition determine the ways in which countries and businesses respond to the international environment.

Learning Objective #3: Discuss the factors involved in deciding to do business internationally and in selecting the appropriate levels of international involvement and international organizational structure.

Learning Objective #4: Describe some of the ways in which social, cultural, economic, legal, and political differences among nations affect international business.

Critical Thinking Questions

1. Why is it important for companies with international operations to observe exchange-rate fluctuations?

2. What factors influence the success of an international operation?

Brain Teaser

What concerns are raised by critics of globalization?

ANSWERS

True-False—Answers

1. False: The contemporary world economy revolves around three major marketplaces: *North America, Europe,* and *Asia.*
2. True
3. True
4. False: The *balance of trade* refers to the amount of goods a nation imports and exports; the b*alance of payments* refers to the amount of money flowing in and out of the country.
5. False: A strong dollar would *decrease* U.S. exports and *increase* its imports.
6. True
7. True
8. True
9. True
10. False: *Foreign Direct Investment (FDI)* is the investment of money by foreign companies in domestic business enterprises.
11. False: Cultural differences *are very important* when doing international business.
12. True
13. True
14. False: A *tariff* is a tax on an imported product; a *quota* is a limit on the quantity allowed to enter the country.
15. True
16. True
17. True

Multiple Choice—Answers

1. d	3. c	5. b	7. c	9. b	11. c
2. a	4. c	6. b	8. d	10. c	12. a

Match the Terms and Concepts with Their Definitions—Answers

1. d	6. ee	11. k	16. a	21. c	26. e	31. z
2. o	7. q	12. cc	17. t	22. w	27. dd	
3. v	8. g	13. x	18. bb	23. aa	28. m	
4. h	9. b	14. i	19. r	24. l	29. s	
5. f	10. u	15. n	20. j	25. y	30. p	

Jeopardy—Answers

International Business	Import-Export Balances	International Organizational Structures
What is globalization?	What is a trade deficit?	What is an independent agent?
What are imports?	What is a balance of payments?	What is a strategic alliance?
What are exports?	What is the exchange rate?	What is a licensing agreement?

Learning Objectives—Short Answer or Essay Questions—Answers

Learning Objective #1: Discuss the rise of international business and describe the major world marketplaces and trade agreements and alliances.
The term *globalization* refers to the process by which the world economy is fast becoming a single interdependent system. The three major marketplaces for international business are *North America*, *Europe*, and *Asia*.

Various legal agreements have sparked international trade and shape the global business environment. A *treaty* is a legal agreement that specifies areas in which nations will cooperate with one another. Among the most significant treaties is the North American Free Trade Agreement. The European Union, the Association of Southeast Asian Nations, and the World Trade Organization are also instrumental in promoting international business.

Learning Objective #2: Explain how differences in import-export balances, exchange rates, and foreign competition determine the ways in which countries and businesses respond to the international environment.
A nation's *balance of trade* is the total economic value of all products that it exports minus the total economic value of all products that it imports. When a country's imports exceed its exports—when it has a *negative balance of trade*—it suffers a *trade deficit*; a *positive balance of trade* occurs when exports exceed imports, resulting in a *trade surplus*. The *balance of payments* refers to the flow of money into or out of a country.

An *exchange rate* is the rate at which one nation's currency can be exchanged for that of another. Under *floating exchange rates*, the value of one currency relative to that of another varies with market conditions.

Countries export what they can produce better or less expensively than other countries and use the proceeds to import what they can't produce as effectively. Economists once focused on two forms of advantage to explain international trade: *absolute advantage* and *comparative advantage*. Today, the theory of *national competitive advantage* is a widely accepted model of why nations engage in international trade.

Learning Objective #3: Discuss the factors involved in deciding to do business internationally and in selecting the appropriate levels of international involvement and international organizational structure.

In deciding whether to do business internationally, a firm must determine whether a market for its product exists abroad and, if so, whether it has the skills and knowledge to manage such a business. It must also assess the business climates of other nations to make sure that they are conducive to international operations. A firm must also decide on its level of international involvement. It can choose to be an *exporter* or *importer*, to organize as an *international firm*, or to operate as a *multifunctional firm*. The choice influences the structure of its international operations, specifically its use of *independent agents*, *licensing arrangements*, *branch offices*, *strategic alliances*, and *direct investment*.

Learning Objective #4: Describe some of the ways in which social, cultural, economic, legal, and political differences among nations affect international business.

Social and cultural differences that can serve as barriers to trade include language, social values, and traditional buying patterns. Differences in economic systems may force businesses to establish close relationships with foreign governments before they are permitted to do business abroad. *Quotas*, *tariffs*, *subsidies*, and *local content laws* offer protection to local industries. Differences in *business practice laws* can make standard business practices in one nation illegal in another.

Critical Thinking Questions—Answers

1. **Why is it important for companies with international operations to observe exchange-rate fluctuations?**
   Companies with international operations must watch exchange-rate fluctuations closely because changes affect overseas demand for their products and can be a major factor in competition.

2. **What factors influence the success of an international operation?**
   Any firm planning to conduct business abroad must understand the social and cultural differences between the host country and home country.

Brain Teaser—Answer

What concerns are raised by critics of globalization?

Globalization is not without its detractors. Some critics charge that globalization allows businesses to exploit workers in less developed countries and bypass domestic environmental and tax regulations. They also charge that globalization leads to the loss of cultural heritages and often benefits the rich more than the poor.

Chapter 5
Business Management

Learning Objectives

After reading this chapter, you should be able to:

1. Describe the nature of management and identify the four basic functions that constitute the management process.
2. Identify different types of managers likely to be found in an organization by level and area.
3. Describe the basic skills required of managers.
4. Explain the importance of strategic management and effective goal setting in organizational success.
5. Discuss contingency planning and crisis management in today's business world.
6. Describe the development and explain the importance of corporate culture.

True-False

Indicate whether the statement is generally true or false by placing a "T" or an "F" in the space provided. If it is a false statement, correct it so that it becomes a true statement.

_____ 1. A statement of an organization's purpose is known as a vision.

_____ 2. Regardless of a company's purpose and mission, every firm has long-term, intermediate, and short-term goals.

_____ 3. Strategic goals are really long-term goals derived from a firm's mission statement.

_____ 4. Environmental analysis studies the strengths and weaknesses within a firm, whereas organizational analysis involves scanning the external environment for threats and weaknesses.

_____ 5. Typically, top managers develop strategic plans, middle managers develop tactical plans, and first-line managers develop operational plans.

_____ 6. Tactical plans are plans that define the actions and the resource allocations necessary to achieve strategic objectives.

_____ 7. The four management functions are planning, organizing, firing, and controlling.

_____ 8. The three basic levels of management are top, middle, and first-line management.

_____ 9.   First-line managers are those at the top of the organization's management
             hierarchy.

_____ 10. Middle managers develop plans to implement the goals of top managers and
             coordinate the work of first-line managers.

_____ 11. In addition to setting goals and assuming various roles, managers also employ
             skills that fall into five basic categories: technical, human relations,
             conceptual, decision making, and time management.

_____ 12. Human relations skills are the ability to perform the mechanics of a job.

_____ 13. Top managers depend most on conceptual skills, while first-line managers
             depend on these skills the least.

_____ 14. Managers of the future will need to understand foreign markets, cultural
             differences, and the motives and practices of foreign rivals.

_____ 15. Corporate culture has little influence on management philosophy, style,
             and behavior.

_____ 16. Corporate culture is the shared experiences, stories, beliefs, and norms that
             characterize an organization.

_____ 17. Once a corporate culture has been established, it doesn't change.

_____ 18. If a corporate culture is altered, it must be communicated to all stakeholders.

Multiple Choice

Circle the best answer for each of the following questions.

1. Company goals
   a.   provide direction and guidance for managers at all levels.
   b.   reduce the firm's ability to allocate resources.
   c.   confuse the sense of corporate culture.
   d.   make it more difficult for managers to assess performance.

2. A goal set for a period of 1 to 5 years is
   a.   an immediate goal.
   b.   a short-term goal.
   c.   an intermediate goal.
   d.   a long-term goal.

3. Which of the following is *true* about plans?
   a. Strategic plans, which are developed by mid- and lower-level managers, set short-term targets for daily, weekly, or monthly performance.
   b. Tactical plans are shorter-range plans for implementing specific aspects of the company's strategic plans.
   c. Operational plans reflect decisions about resource allocations, company priorities, and the steps needed to meet long-term company objectives.
   d. All of the above.

4. Which type of plan do top managers usually develop?
   a. Operational plans
   b. Strategic plans
   c. Tactical plans
   d. Forecasting plans

5. The management process that monitors progress toward company goals, resets the course if goals or objectives change, and corrects deviations if goals or objectives are not being attained is called the
   a. planning function of management.
   b. organizing function of management.
   c. controlling function of management.
   d. directing function of management.

6. The order in which plans are undertaken is
   a. tactical, operational, and then strategic.
   b. strategic, tactical, and then operational.
   c. operational, strategic, and then tactical.
   d. operational, tactical, and then strategic.

7. Middle managers
   a. are responsible for the overall performance and effectiveness of the firm.
   b. spend most of their time working with and supervising employees at the bottom of the organization.
   c. set strategic goals and direct the firm toward the realization of its mission statement.
   d. are responsible for implementing the strategies, policies, and decisions made by top managers.

8. Managers who hire and train employees, who evaluate performance, and who determine compensation are
   a. human resource managers.
   b. operations managers.
   c. finance managers.
   d. information managers.

9. The skill that enables a manager to think in the abstract, to diagnose and analyze different situations, and to see beyond the present situation is a
   a. technical skill.
   b. time management skill.
   c. decision-making skill.
   d. conceptual skill.

10. Skills especially important for first-line managers are
    a. technical skills.   b. time management skills.
    c. decision-making skills.   d. conceptual skills.

11. Decision making involves
    a. defining the problem, gathering the facts, and identifying alternative solutions.
    b. evaluating alternative solutions and selecting the best one.
    c. implementing a chosen alternative and periodically following up and evaluating
        the effectiveness of that choice.
    d. All of the above.

12. Which of the following is a leading causes of wasted time, reducing managers' ability
    to manage their time effectively?
    a. Telephone calls and e-mails   b. Meetings
    c.   Paperwork   d. All of the above.

13. To use a firm's culture to its advantage, managers
    a. must have a clear understanding of the culture.
    b. must transmit the culture to others in the organization.
    c. need to reward and promote those who understand the culture and work toward
        maintaining it.
    d. All of the above.

14. Which of the following is an effective way management could deal with radical
    change within an organization?
    a. Top management highlights extensive change as the most effective response to
        the company's problems.
    b. Top management resists change in the company's vision or culture.
    c. Top management maintains the company's original system of appraising and
        compensating employees.
    d. All of the above.

Match the Terms and Concepts with Their Definitions

a. goal   i. organizational analysis   q. top managers
b. mission statement   j. strategic plans   r. middle managers
c. long-term goals   k. tactical plans   s. first-line managers
d. intermediate goals   l. operational plans   t. technical skills
e. short-term goals   m. management   u. human relations skills
f. strategy formulation   n. planning   v. conceptual skills
g. strategic goals   o. organizing   w. decision-making skills
h. environmental analysis   p. controlling   x. corporate culture

_____ 1. Goals set for a period of 1 to 5 years into the future.

_____ 2. The management process of monitoring an organization's performance to ensure that it is meeting its goals.

_____ 3. The management process of determining what an organization needs to do and how best to get it done.

_____ 4. The skills in defining problems and selecting the best courses of action.

_____ 5. The process of analyzing a firm's strengths and weaknesses.

_____ 6. The skills needed to perform specialized tasks.

_____ 7. Managers that report to the board of directors and stockholders and are responsible for a firm's overall performance and effectiveness.

_____ 8. The shared experiences, stories, beliefs, and norms that characterize an organization.

_____ 9. An organization's statement of how it will achieve its purpose in the environment in which it conducts its business.

_____ 10. The creation of a broad program for defining and meeting an organization's goals.

_____ 11. The process of planning, organizing, directing, and controlling an organization's resources in order to achieve its goals.

_____ 12. Managers responsible for implementing the strategies, policies, and decisions made by top managers.

_____ 13. An objective that a business hopes and plans to achieve.

_____ 14. Managers responsible for supervising the work of employees.

_____ 15. Generally short-range plans concerned with implementing specific aspects of a company's strategic plans.

_____ 16. The long-term goals derived directly from a firm's mission statement.

_____ 17. The skills necessary for understanding and getting along with people.

_____ 18. The management process of determining how best to arrange an organization's resources and activities into a coherent structure.

_____ 19. The ability to think in the abstract, diagnose, and analyze different situations, and see beyond the present situation.

_____ 20. The process of scanning the business environment for threats and opportunities.

_____ 21. The goals set for an extended time, typically 5 years or more into the future.

_____ 22. The goals set for the near future, typically less than 1 year.

_____ 23. Plans setting short-term targets for daily, weekly, or monthly performance.

_____ 24. Plans reflecting decisions about resource allocations, company priorities, and steps needed to meet strategic goals.

Let's List

1. What are the three different types of strategies typically used by firms today?
   a. _____
   b. _____
   c. _____

2. What are four purposes in organizational goal setting?
   a. _____
   b. _____
   c. _____
   d. _____

3. What are three levels of plans managers can use?
   a. _____
   b. _____
   c. _____

4. List six different areas of management commonly used.
   a. _____   d. _____
   b. _____   e. _____
   c. _____   f. _____

Learning Objectives—Short Answer or Essay Questions

Learning Objective #1: Describe the nature of management and identify the four basic functions that constitute the management process.

Learning Objective #2: Identify different types of managers likely to be found in an organization by level and area.

Learning Objective #3: Describe the basic skills required of managers.

Learning Objective #4: Explain the importance of strategic management and effective goal setting in organizational success.

Learning Objective #5: Discuss contingency planning and crisis management in today's business world.

Learning Objective #6: Describe the development and explain the importance of corporate culture.

Critical Thinking Questions

1. What role do information managers play in the area of management?

2. Why are conceptual skills important as a basic management skill?

Brain Teaser

Why is contingency planning important to managers?

ANSWERS

True-False—Answers

1. False: A statement of an organization's purpose is known as a *mission statement*.
2. True
3. True
4. False: *Organizational analysis* studies the strengths and weaknesses within a firm, whereas *environmental analysis* involves scanning the external environment for threats and weaknesses.
5. True
6. False: *Strategic* plans are plans that define the actions and the resource allocation necessary to achieve strategic objectives.
7. False: The four management functions are planning, organizing, *directing*, and controlling.
8. True
9. False: First-line managers are those at the *bottom* of the organization's management hierarchy.
10. True
11. True
12. False: *Technical skills* are the ability to perform the mechanics of a job.
13. True
14. True
15. False: Corporate culture has *a big* influence on management philosophy, style, and behavior.
16. True
17. False: Sometimes a corporate culture must be updated, altered, or otherwise adjusted.
18. True

Multiple Choice—Answers

1. a	3. b	5. c	7. d	9. d	11. d	13. d
2. c	4. b	6. b	8. a	10. a	12. d	14. a

Match the Terms and Concepts with Their Definitions—Answers

1. d	6. t	11. m	16. g	21. c
2. p	7. q	12. r	17. u	22. e
3. n	8. x	13. a	18. o	23. 1
4. w	9. b	14. s	19. v	24. j
5. i	10. f	15. k	20. h	

Let's List—Answers

1. What are the three different types of strategies typically used by firms today?
   a. Corporate strategy
   b. Business or competitive strategy
   c. Functional strategy

2. What are four purposes in organizational goal setting?
   a. Goal setting provides direction and guidance for managers at all levels.
   b. Goal setting helps firms allocate resources.
   c. Goal setting helps to define corporate culture.
   d. Goal setting helps managers assess performance.

3. What are three levels of plans managers can use?
   a. Strategic
   b. Tactical
   c. Operational

4. List six different areas of management commonly used.
   a. Human resource managers
   b. Operations managers
   c. Marketing managers
   d. Information managers
   e. Financial managers
   f. Specialized managers

Learning Objectives—Short Answer or Essay Questions—Answers

Learning Objective #1: Describe the nature of management and identify the four basic functions that constitute the management process.
Management is the process of planning, organizing, leading, and controlling all of a firm's resources to achieve its goals. *Planning* is determining what the organization needs to do and how best to get it done. The process of arranging resources and activities into a coherent structure is called *organizing*. When *leading*, a manager guides and motivates employees to meet the firm's objectives. *Controlling* is the process of monitoring performance to make sure that a firm is meeting its goals.

Learning Objective #2: Identify different types of managers likely to be found in an organization by level and area.
There are three levels of management. The few executives who are responsible for the overall performance of large companies are top managers. Just below top managers are middle managers, who implement strategies, policies, and decisions made by top managers. Supervisors and office managers are the first-line managers who work with and supervise the employees who report to them.

In any large company, most managers work in one of five areas. Human resource managers hire and train employees, assess performance, and fix compensation. Operations managers are responsible for production, inventory, and quality control. Marketing managers are responsible for getting products from producers to consumers. Information managers design and implement systems to gather, organize, and distribute information. Some firms have a top manager called a chief information officer (CIO). Financial managers, including the chief financial officer (top), division controllers (middle), and accounting supervisors (first-line), oversee accounting functions and financial resources.

Learning Objective #3: Describe the basic skills required of managers.
Effective managers must develop a number of important skills. Technical skills are skills needed to perform specialized tasks. Human relations skills are skills necessary for understanding and getting along with other people. Conceptual skills refer to the ability to think abstractly as well as diagnose and analyze different situations. Decision-making skills include the ability to define problems and select the best courses of action. Time management skills refer to the productive use of time. Global management skills include understanding foreign markets, cultural differences, and the motives and practices of foreign rivals. Technology management skills include the ability to process, organize, and interpret an ever-increasing amount of information.

Learning Objective #4: Explain the importance of strategic management and effective goal setting in organizational success.
Strategic management is the process of helping an organization maintain an effective alignment with its environment. It starts with setting goals—objectives that a business hopes (and plans) to achieve. Determined by the board and top management, strategies reflect decisions about resource allocations, company priorities, and plans. The three types of strategy that are usually considered by a company are *corporate strategy*, *business* (or *competitive*) *strategy*, and *functional strategy*.

Learning Objective #5: Discuss contingency planning and crisis management in today's business world.
Companies often develop alternative plans in case things go awry. There are two common methods of dealing with the unforeseen: contingency planning and crisis management. *Contingency planning* is planning for change. It seeks to identify, in advance, important aspects of a business or its market that might change. It also identifies the ways in which a company will respond to changes. *Crisis management* involves an organization's methods for dealing with emergencies.

Learning Objective #6: Describe the development and explain the importance of corporate culture.
Every company has a unique identity called corporate culture: its shared experiences, stories, beliefs, and norms. It helps define the work and business climate of an organization. A strong corporate culture directs efforts and helps everyone work toward the same goals. If an organization must change its culture, it must communicate the nature of the change to both employees and customers.

Critical Thinking Questions—Answers

1. **What role do information managers play in the area of management?**
   Occupying a fairly new managerial position in many firms, information managers design and implement systems to gather, organize, and distribute information. Some firms have a top-management position for a chief information officer (CIO).

2. **Why are conceptual skills as important as a basic management skill?**
   Conceptual skills refer to a person's ability to think in the abstract, to diagnose and analyze different situations, and to see beyond the present situation.

Brain Teaser—Answer

Why is contingency planning important to managers?

Contingency planning seeks to identify in advance important aspects of a business or its market that might change. It also identifies the ways in which a company will respond to changes.

Chapter 6
Organizing the Business

Learning Objectives
After reading this chapter, you should be able to:

1. Discuss the factors that influence a firm's organizational structure.
2. Explain specialization and departmentalization as two of the building blocks of organizational structure.
3. Describe centralization and decentralization, delegation, and authority as the key ingredients in establishing the decision-making hierarchy.
4. Explain the differences among functional, divisional, matrix, and international organizational structures and describe the most popular new forms of organizational design.
5. Describe the informal organization and discuss intrapreneuring.

True-False
Indicate whether the statement is generally true or false by placing a "T" or an "F" in the space provided. If it is a false statement, correct it so that it becomes a true statement.

_____ 1. Key elements that work together in determining an organization's structure include the organization's purpose, mission, and strategy.

_____ 2. An organization chart depicts a company's structure and shows employees where they fit into its operations.

_____ 3. The first step in developing the structure of any business, large or small, involves two activities: specialization and departmentalization.

_____ 4. Specialization involves determining how people performing certain tasks can best be grouped together; departmentalization involves determining who will do what.

_____ 5. Rarely do companies adopt different forms of departmentalization for their various levels of organization.

_____ 6. After jobs have been appropriately specialized and grouped into manageable departments, the next step in organizing is to establish the decision-making hierarchy.

_____ 7. *Authority* is the duty to perform an assigned task; *responsibility* is the power to make the decisions necessary to complete the task.

_____ 8. Accountability begins when a manager assigns a task to a subordinate; delegation falls to subordinates, who must then complete the task.

_____ 9. In a decentralized organization, upper-level managers hold most decision-making authority.

_____ 10. With relatively fewer layers of management, decentralized firms tend to reflect a tall organizational structure.

_____ 11. A flat organization has a narrow span of management and many layers of management.

_____ 12. When a large number of people report directly to one person, that person has a wide span of management control.

_____ 13. Three forms of authority are line authority, staff authority, and committee and team authority.

_____ 14. The four most common forms of organizational structure are the functional, divisional, matrix, and international structures.

_____ 15. A functional organization relies on product departmentalization.

_____ 16. Functional organization is the approach to organizational structure used by most small to medium-sized firms.

_____ 17. In a matrix organizational structure, teams are formed in which individuals report to two or more managers.

_____ 18. There are many specific types of international organizational structures.

_____ 19. Formal organization refers to the everyday social interactions among employees that transcend formal jobs and job interrelationships.

_____ 20. Internal communication networks involve both formal and informal communication channels.

_____ 21. Intrapreneuring is the process of creating and maintaining the innovation and flexibility of a small-business environment within the confines of a large organization.

_____ 22. Regardless of how an organization divides its tasks, it will function more smoothly if employees are clear about who is responsible for each task, and who has the authority to make official decisions.

_____ 23. Many managers know informal communication exists and try to work with it.

Multiple Choice

Circle the best answer for each of the following questions.

1. Which of the following is *true*?
   a. *Chain of command* refers to the reporting relationships within a company.
   b. Job specialization is a natural consequence of organizational growth.
   c. After jobs are specialized, they must be grouped into logical units, which is the process of departmentalization.
   d. All of the above.

2. Which of the following is NOT a form of departmentalization?
   a. Internal departmentalization
   b. Customer departmentalization
   c. Product departmentalization
   d. Functional departmentalization

3. Departmentalization according to types of customers likely to buy a given product is
   a. product departmentalization.
   b. geographic departmentalization.
   c. customer departmentalization.
   d. functional departmentalization.

4. Departmentalization according to groups' activities is
   a. process departmentalization.
   b. geographic departmentalization.
   c. customer departmentalization.
   d. functional departmentalization.

5. Departmentalization
   a. can occur by function, geography, process, product, or customer.
   b. by process requires the same equipment and the same worker skills when producing different products.
   c. by geography is dividing the company according to the specific product or service being created.
   d. All of the above.

6. Establishing the decision-making hierarchy involves
   a. assigning tasks.
   b. performing tasks.
   c. distributing authority.
   d. All of the above.

7. Which of the following statements is *true*?
   a. Authority is the power to make decisions necessary to complete a task.
   b. Delegation is the obligation to complete a task.
   c. Accountability is the duty to perform an assigned task.
   d. Responsibility is assigning a task to a subordinate.

8. To overcome the problems associated with a lack of delegating, managers should
   a. recognize that if they want the job done right, they should do it themselves.
   b. stop training workers where the training increases workers' responsibilities.
   c. recognize that if a subordinate performs well, it reflects favorably on themselves.
   d. All of the above.

9. Which of the following statements is *true*?
    a. A flat organization has a narrow span and many layers of management.
    b. Decentralized firms tend to reflect a flat organizational structure.
    c. If a manager has few people reporting directly to him or her, the manager has a wide span of management.
    d. All of the above.

10. Which of the following statements is *true*?
    a. The line-and-staff organization system has a clear chain of command, but also includes groups of people who provide advice and specialized services.
    b. When several employees perform either the same simple task or a group of interrelated tasks, a wide span of control is possible and often desirable.
    c. A profit center is a separate unit responsible for its own cost and profits.
    d. All of the above.

11. Which of the following statements is *true*?
    a. No formula exists for determining the ideal span of management control.
    b. Organizations that focus decision-making authority near the top of the chain of command are said to be decentralized.
    c. The most complicated chain of command is the line authority organization.
    d. All of the above.

12. An organizational structure in which corporate divisions operate as autonomous businesses under the larger corporate umbrella is
    a. a functional organization.   b. a matrix structure.
    c. a divisional organization.   d. an international organizational structure.

13. In a matrix organizational structure
    a. one manager has functional expertise, while the others have project orientation.
    b. flexibility exists, which allows for ready adaptability to changing circumstances.
    c. people rely on committee and team authority.
    d. All of the above.

14. Which of the following is *true*?
    a. The team organization involves continuous employee learning and development.
    b. The virtual organization has little or no formal organization.
    c. The learning organization has traditional territories minimized or eliminated.
    d. None of the above.

15. Which of the following is *true*?
    a. The grapevine is an informal communication network.
    b. Frequently, informal organization effectively alters a company's formal structure.
    c. Intrapreneuring is the process of creating and maintaining the innovation and flexibility of a small-business environment within the confines of a large organization.
    d. All of the above.

Match the Terms and Concepts with Their Definitions

a. organizational structure

b. organization chart

c. chain of command

d. job specialization

e. departmentalization

f. profit center

g. customer departmentalization

h. product departmentalization

i. process departmentalization

j. geographic departmentalization

k. functional departmentalization

l. responsibility

m. authority

n. delegation

o. accountability

p. centralized organization

q. decentralized organization

r. flat organizational structure

s. tall organizational structure

t. span of control

u. line authority

v. line department

w. staff authority

x staff members

y. committee and team authority

z. functional structure

aa. divisional structure

bb. division

cc. matrix structure

dd. international organizational structure

ee. informal organization

ff. intrapreneuring

_____ 1. A department that resembles a separate business in producing its own products.

_____ 2. A characteristic of centralized companies with multiple layers of management and relatively narrow spans of control.

_____ 3. Departmentalization according to groups' functions or activities.

_____ 4. The process of identifying the specific jobs that need to be done and designating the people who will perform them.

_____ 5. Departmentalization according to the types of customers likely to buy a product.

_____ 6. A network, unrelated to the firm's formal authority structure, of everyday social interactions among company employees.

_____ 7. Advisors and counselors who aid line departments in making decisions.

_____ 8. The decision-making authority held by upper-level management.

_____ 9. Departmentalization according to production processes used to create a good.

_____ 10. A form of business organization in which authority is determined by the relationships between group functions and activities.

_____ 11. The power to make the decisions necessary to complete a task.

_____ 12. A diagram depicting a company's structure and showing employees where they fit into its operations.

_____ 13. An organizational structure in which authority flows in a direct chain of command from the top of the company to the bottom.

_____ 14. The approaches to organizational structure developed in response to the need to manufacture, purchase, and sell in global markets.

_____ 15. The authority granted to teams involved in a firm's daily operations.

_____ 16. An organization in which a great deal of decision-making authority is delegated to levels of management at points below the top.

_____ 17. The process of grouping jobs into logical units.

_____ 18. The number of people supervised by one manager.

_____ 19. The assignment of a task or responsibility by a manager to a subordinate.

_____ 20. The process of creating and maintaining the innovation and flexibility of a small-business environment within the confines of a large organization.

_____ 21. The organizational structure in which corporate divisions operate as autonomous businesses under the larger corporate umbrella.

_____ 22. Departmentalization according to areas served by a business.

_____ 23. The specification of the jobs to be done within an organization and the ways in which they relate to one another.

_____ 24. A separate company unit responsible for its own costs and profits.

_____ 25. The authority based on expertise that usually involves advising line managers.

_____ 26. An obligation employees have to their manager for the successful completion of an assigned task.

_____ 27. An organizational structure in which teams are formed and team members report to two or more managers.

_____ 28. The department directly linked to the production and sales of a specific product.

_____ 29. Reporting relationships within a company.

_____ 30. Departmentalization according to specific products being created.

_____ 31. A characteristic of decentralized companies with relatively few layers of management and relatively wide spans of control.

_____ 32. The duty to perform an assigned task.

Learning Objectives—Short Answer or Essay Questions

Learning Objective #1: Discuss the factors that influence a firm's organizational structure.

Learning Objective #2: Explain specialization and departmentalization as two of the building blocks of organizational structure.

Learning Objective #3: Describe centralization and decentralization, delegation, and authority as the key ingredients in establishing the decision-making hierarchy.

Learning Objective #4: Explain the differences among functional, divisional, matrix, and international organizational structures and describe the most popular new forms of organizational design.

Learning Objective #5: Describe the informal organization and discuss intrapreneuring.

Critical Thinking Questions

1. How do some companies use staff authority?

2. What factors influence an organization's span of control?

Brain Teaser

What are the challenges in organizational design for the twenty-first century?

ANSWERS

True-False—Answers

1. True
2. True
3. True
4. False: *Departmentalization* is determining how people performing certain tasks can best be grouped together; *specialization* is determining who will do what.
5. False: *Often* companies adopt different forms of departmentalization for their various levels of organization—*especially larger companies.*
6. True
7. False: *Responsibility* is the duty to perform an assigned task; *authority* is the power to make the decisions necessary to complete the task.
8. False: *Delegation* begins when a manager assigns a task to a subordinate; *accountability* falls to subordinates, who must then complete the task.
9. False: In a *centralized* organization, upper-level managers hold most decision-making authority.
10. False: With relatively fewer layers of management, decentralized firms tend to reflect a *flat* organizational structure.
11. False: A *tall* organization has a narrow span and many layers of management.
12. True
13. True
14. True
15. False: A *divisional* organization relies on product departmentalization.
16. True
17. True
18. True
19. False: *Informal* organization is the everyday social interactions among employees that transcend formal jobs and job interrelationships.
20. True
21. True
22. True
23. True

Multiple Choice—Answers

1. d	4. d	7. a	10. d	13. d
2. a	5. a	8. c	11. a	14. b
3. c	6. d	9. b	12. c	15. d

Match the Terms and Concepts with Their Definitions—Answers

1. bb	6. ee	11. m	16. q	21. aa	26. o	31. r
2. s	7. x	12. b	17. e	22. j	27. cc	32. l
3. k	8. p	13. u	18. t	23. a	28. v	
4. d	9. i	14. dd	19. n	24. f	29. c	
5. g	10. z	15. y	20. ff	25. w	30. h	

Learning Objectives—Short Answer or Essay Questions—Answers

Learning Objective #1: Discuss the factors that influence a firm's organizational structure.

Organizational structure varies according to a firm's mission, purpose, and strategy. Size, technology, and changes in environmental circumstances also influence structure. In general, although all organizations have the same basic elements, each develops the structure that contributes to the most efficient operations.

Learning Objective #2: Explain specialization and departmentalization as two of the building blocks of organizational structure.

The building blocks of organizational structure are *job specialization* and *departmentalization*. As a firm grows, it usually has a greater need for people to perform specialized tasks (specialization). It also has a greater need to group types of work into logical units (departmentalization). Common forms of departmentalization are *customer, product, process, geographic,* and *functional*. Large businesses often use more than one form of departmentalization.

Learning Objective #3: Describe centralization and decentralization, delegation, and authority as the key ingredients in establishing the decision-making hierarchy.

After jobs have been specialized and departmentalized, firms establish decision-making hierarchies. *Centralized authority* systems typically require multiple layers of management and thus tall organizational structures. *Decentralized firms* tend to have relatively fewer layers of management, resulting in a flat organizational structure. *Delegation* is the process through which a manager allocates work to subordinates. In general, it involves (1) the assignment of responsibility, (2) the granting of authority, and (3) the creation of accountability. As individuals are delegated responsibility and authority in a firm, a complex web of interactions develops. These interactions may take one of three forms of authority: *line, staff,* or *committee and team*.

Learning Objective #4: Explain the differences among functional, divisional, matrix, and international organizational structures and describe the most popular new forms of organizational design.

In a *functional organization*, authority is usually distributed among such basic functions as marketing and finance. In a *divisional organization*, the various divisions of a larger company, which may be related or unrelated, operate in a relatively autonomous fashion. In *matrix organizations*, in which individuals report to more than one manager, the company creates teams to address specific problems or to conduct specific projects. A company that has divisions in many countries may require an additional level of *international organization* to coordinate those operations.

Learning Objective #5: Describe the informal organization and discuss intrapreneuring.

The *informal organization* consists of the everyday social interactions among employees that transcend formal jobs and job interrelationships. To foster the innovation and flexibility of a small business within the big-business environment, some large companies encourage *intrapreneuring*—creating and maintaining the innovation and flexibility of a small-business environment within the confines of a large bureaucratic structure.

Critical Thinking Questions—Answers

1. **How do some companies use staff authority?**

   Some companies rely on staff authority, which is based on special expertise and usually involves advising line managers in areas such as law, accounting, and human resources. A corporate attorney, for example, may advise the marketing department as it prepares a new contract with the firm's advertising agency, but will not typically make decisions that affect how the marketing department does its job.

2. **What factors influence an organization's span of control?**

   The span of control can be influenced by employees' abilities and the supervisor's managerial skills influence how wide or narrow the span of control should be, as do the similarity and simplicity of tasks and the extent to which they are interrelated.

Brain Teaser—Answer

What are the challenges in organizational design for the twenty-first century?

As the world grows increasingly complex and fast-paced, organizations also continue to seek new forms of organization that permit them to compete effectively. Among the most popular of these new forms are the team organization, the virtual organization, and the learning organization.

Chapter 7
Operations Management and Quality

Learning Objectives
After reading this chapter, you should be able to:

1. Explain the meaning of the term *production* or *operations*.
2. Describe the three kinds of utility that operations processes provide for adding customer value.
3. Explain how companies with different business strategies are best served by having different operations capabilities.
4. Identify the major factors that are considered in operations planning.
5. Discuss the information contained in four kinds of operations schedules—the master production schedule, detailed schedule, staff schedule, and project schedule.
6. Identify the activities involved in operations control.
7. Identify the activities and underlying objectives involved in total quality management.
8. Explain how a supply chain strategy differs from traditional strategies for coordinating operations among firms.

True-False
Indicate whether the statement is generally true or false by placing a "T" or an "F" in the space provided. If it is a false statement, correct it so that it becomes a true statement.

_____ 1. The term *operations* refers to all the activities involved in making products—goods and services—for customers.

_____ 2. The four kinds of utility that products create for customers are time, place, ownership, and space utility.

_____ 3. Time utility refers to consumer satisfaction derived from a product being available where it is most convenient for the customer.

_____ 4. Make-to-order operations produce a one-of-a-kind product.

_____ 5. Make-to-stock operations produce standard products in large quantities to be stocked on store shelves or in displays for mass consumption.

_____ 6. Service operations are classified according to the extent of customer contact.

_____ 7. A high-contact service operations process is one in which the customer need not be part of the system to receive the service.

_____ 8. Two prominent characteristics—*intangibility* and *unstorability*—set services apart from physical goods.

_____ 9. Service providers typically focus on the customer service link, often acknowledging the customer as part of the operations process.

_____ 10. Operations planning activities fall into five main categories: *capacity*, *location*, *layout*, *quality*, and *methods planning*.

_____ 11. Capacity planning for goods means ensuring that a manufacturing firm's capacity is slightly below the normal demand for its product.

_____ 12. Location planning for low-contact services focuses on locating the service near customers who are part of the system.

_____ 13. Process flow charts are helpful for identifying all operations activities and eliminating wasteful steps from production.

_____ 14. The ISO 14000 program certifies improvements in environmental performance.

_____ 15. A master production schedule shows which products will be produced, when production will occur, and what resources will be used during specified time periods.

_____ 16. Follow-up is an essential and ongoing facet of operations control.

_____ 17. Just-in-time production systems are concerned with planning, organizing, and controlling the flow of materials.

_____ 18. Just-in-time systems are more susceptible to disruptions in the flow of raw materials but allow for disruptions to get resolved more quickly.

_____ 19. In just-in-time production, raw materials are brought together at least two months in advance of the product being made.

_____ 20. The five main areas in materials management are supplier selection, purchasing, transportation, warehousing, and inventory control.

_____ 21. Total quality management (TQM) is the planning, organizing, directing, and controlling of the activities needed to get high-quality goods and services into the marketplace.

_____ 22. Planning for quality begins after products are designed or redesigned.

_____ 23. Performance is a dimension of quality that refers to sameness of product quality from unit to unit.

_____ 24. Quality ownership is the principle of total quality management that holds that quality belongs to each person who creates it while performing a job.

_____ 25. Staff schedules specify assigned working times for only the upcoming week, for each employee on each work shift.

_____ 26. Value-added analysis refers to the evaluation of all work activities, material flows, and paperwork to determine the value that they add for customers.

_____ 27. "Getting closer to the consumer" is a total quality management tool that provides firms with a better understanding of what consumers want so that they can satisfy them more effectively.

_____ 28. Supply chain management looks at the supply chain as a whole in order to improve the overall flow through the system.

_____ 29. The efficiency of supply chain management means faster deliveries and lower costs than customers could get otherwise.

Multiple Choice
Circle the best answer for each of the following questions:

1. Which of the following statements is *true*?
   a. Production and employment in the services sector of our economy has been rising more rapidly than in the goods sector.
   b. Resources are those things used in the production of goods and services.
   c. Utility is a product's ability to satisfy a human want.
   d. All of the above.

2. Which of the following is a resource?
   a. Knowledge   b. Raw materials and equipment
   c. Labor   d. All of the above.

3. Which of the following is NOT one of the kinds of utility goods and services provide to customers?
   a. Form   b. Leisure
   c. Place   d. Time

4. The satisfaction derived by having a product available where it is convenient for customers is
   a. time utility.
   b. form utility.
   c. place utility.
   d. ownership utility.

5. Services, as opposed to goods, are
   a. largely intangible.
   b. are performed rather than produced.
   c. more unstorable.
   d. All of the above.

6. Which of the following statements are *true*?
   a. Operations managers are responsible for ensuring that operations processes create what customers want and need.
   b. Consumers use different measures to judge services and goods because services include intangibles, not just physical objects.
   c. A high-contact service system exists when the customer is part of the system.
   d. All of the above.

7. The spatial arrangement of production activities designed to move resources through a smooth, fixed sequence of steps is
   a. product layout.
   b. forecasting.
   c. location planning.
   d. quality planning.

8. Capacity planning
   a. is a facet of a production plan that predicts future demand.
   b. for goods means ensuring that a manufacturing firm's capacity meets the normal demand for its product.
   c. considers both current and future requirements.
   d. All of the above.

9. Which of the following is *true*?
   a. Supply chain management looks at the chain as a whole in order to improve the overall flow through a system composed of companies working together.
   b. Supply chain management reduces unwanted inventories, avoids delays, and cuts supply times.
   c. In supply chain management, materials move faster to business customers and individual consumers.
   d. All the above.

10. Planning, organizing, and controlling the flow of materials from design through distribution of finished goods is
    a. purchasing.
    b. follow-up.
    c. materials management.
    d. warehousing.

11. Within a business, the storage of both incoming materials for production and finished goods for distribution to customers is the function of
    a. the transportation department.
    b. the purchasing department.
    b. the warehousing department.
    d. the inventory control department.

12. Management of the production process designed to manufacture goods or supply
    services that meet specific standards is
    a.   bill of materials control.   b.   supplier selection control.
    c.   quality control.   d.   inventory control.

13. A system for determining the right quantity of various items to have on hand and
    keeping track of their location, use, and condition is called
    a.   supply chain management.   b.   inventory control.
    c.   purchasing.   d.   lead time.

14. Just-in-time (JIT) systems attempt to reduce waste and improve quality by
    a.   ordering supplies only when they are needed.
    b.   holding a sufficient buffer stock of inventory to handle unforeseen
         circumstances.
    c.   increasing finished-goods inventory to ensure that only non-defects will be
         shipped to customers.
    d.   All of the above.

15. Which of the following is *not* part of total quality management?
    a.   Planning for quality   b.   Organizing for quality
    c.   Advertising for quality   d.   Directing for quality

16. The total quality management approach requires
    a.   performance quality, quality reliability, and quality ownership.
    b.   the belief that producing high-quality goods and services is an effort that must
         be undertaken by all parts of the organization.
    c.   managers to motivate employees throughout the company to achieve quality
         goals.
    d.   All of the above.

17. A Gantt chart
    a.   begins with raw-materials suppliers.
    b.   refers to the group of companies and stream of activities that operate together to
         create a product.
    c.   continues through stages in the operations process until the product reaches the
         end customer.
    d.   breaks down large projects into steps to be performed and specifies the time
         required to perform each one.

Match the Terms and Concepts with Their Definitions

a. service operations
b. goods production
c. utility

d. operations (production) management
e. operations managers
f. value added analysis
g. Gantt chart

h. high-contact system

i. low-contact system

j. operations process

k. capacity
l. process layout
m. product layout

n. assembly line

o. purchasing
p. operations capability
q. competitive product analysis
r. business process reengineering

s. master production schedule

t. operations control

u. follow-up
v. materials management
w. quality improvement team

x. supplier selection

y. inventory control
z. just-in-time (JIT)
aa. ISO 14000

bb. detailed schedule

cc. total quality management (TQM)

dd. quality control

_____ 1.   Reveals wasteful or unnecessary activities that can be eliminated without jeopardizing customer service.

_____ 2.   A spatial arrangement of production activities designed to move resources through a smooth, fixed sequence of steps.

_____ 3.   A certification program attesting to the fact that a factory, laboratory, or office has improved its environmental performance.

_____ 4.   A schedule showing which products will be produced, when production will take place, and what resources will be used.

_____ 5.   Produces tangible products, such as radios, newspapers, buses, and textbooks.

_____ 6.   The sum of all activities involved in getting high-quality products into the marketplace.

_____ 7.   Planning, organizing, and controlling the flow of materials from design through the distribution of finished goods.

_____ 8.   The acquisition of the materials and services that a firm needs to produce its products.

_____ 9.   The level of customer contact in which the customer need not be a part of the system to receive the service.

_____ 10. In materials management, receiving, storing, handling, and counting of all raw materials, partly finished goods, and finished goods.

_____ 11. The process by which the company analyzes a competitor's products to identify desirable improvements.

_____ 12. The systematic direction and control of the processes that transform resources into finished products.

_____ 13. The amount of a product that a company can produce under normal working conditions.

_____ 14. The activity or process that production must do especially well, and with a high level of proficiency.

_____ 15. The production method that brings together all materials and parts needed at each production stage at the precise moment they are required.

_____ 16. The process of monitoring production performance by comparing results with plans.

_____ 17. The rethinking and radical redesign of business processes to improve performance, quality, and productivity.

_____ 18. A product's ability to satisfy a human want.

_____ 19. The level of customer contact in which the customer is part of the system during service delivery.

_____ 20. Product layout in which a product moves step-by-step through a plant on conveyor belts or other equipment until it is completed.

_____ 21. A schedule showing daily work assignments with start and stop times for assigned jobs.

_____ 22. Produces tangible and intangible services, such as entertainment, transportation, and education.

_____ 23. A tool in which collaborative groups of employees from various work areas work together to improve quality by solving commonly shared production problems.

_____ 24. A set of methods used in the production of a good or service.

_____ 25. Managers responsible for production, inventory, and quality control.

_____ 26. Management of the production process designed to manufacture goods or supply services that meet specific quality standards.

_____ 27. The control activity for ensuring that production decisions are being implemented.

_____ 28. A spatial arrangement of production activities that groups equipment and people according to function.

_____ 29. The production schedule that breaks down large projects into steps to be performed and specifies the time required to perform each step.

_____ 30. The process of finding and selecting suppliers from whom to buy.

Learning Objectives—Short Answer or Essay Questions

Learning Objective #1: Explain the meaning of the term *production* or *operations*.

Learning Objective #2: Describe the three kinds of utility that operations processes provide for adding customer value.

Learning Objective #3: Explain how companies with different business strategies are best served by having different operations capabilities.

Learning Objective #5: Discuss the information contained in four kinds of operations schedules—the master production schedule, detailed schedule, staff schedule, and project schedule.

Learning Objective #6: Identify the activities involved in operations control.

Learning Objective #7: Identify the activities and underlying objectives involved in total quality management.

Learning Objective #8: Explain how a supply chain strategy differs from traditional strategies for coordinating operations among firms.

Critical Thinking Questions

1. Explain how managers use operations control.

2. How do managers motivate employees throughout the company and its suppliers to achieve quality goals?

Brain Teaser

How do managers go about designing operations systems?

ANSWERS

True-False—Answers

1. True
2. False: Utilities that products create for customers are time, place, ownership, and *form* utility.
3. False: Time utility refers to consumer satisfaction derived from a product being available *when* it is most convenient for the customer.
4. True
5. True
6. True
7. False: A *low*-contact service operations process is one in which the customer need not be part of the system to receive the service.
8. True
9. True
10. True
11. False: Capacity planning for goods means ensuring that manufacturing capacity is slightly *above* the normal demand for its product.
12. False: Location planning for *high*-contact services focuses on locating the service near customers who are part of the system.
13. True
14. True
15. True
16. True
17. False: *Materials management* is concerned with planning, organizing, and controlling the flow of materials.
18. True
19. False: It happens immediately.
20. True
21. True
22. False: Planning for quality begins *before* products are designed or redesigned.
23. False: *Performance* is a dimension of quality that refers to *how well a product does what it is supposed to do*; *consistency* is a dimension of quality that refers to sameness of product quality from unit to unit
24. True
25. False: Staff schedules can be created for up to 30 days.
26. True
27. True
28. True
29. True

Multiple Choice—Answers

1. d	4. c	7. a	10. c	13. b	16. d
2. d	5. d	8. d	11. b	14. a	17. d
3. b	6. d	9. d	12. c	15. c	

Match the Terms and Concepts with Their Definitions—Answers

1. f	6. cc	11. q	16. t	21. bb	26. dd
2. m	7. v	12. d	17. r	22. a	27. u
3. aa	8. o	13. k	18. c	23. w	28. l
4. s	9. i	14. p	19. h	24. j	29. g
5. b	10. y	15. z	20. n	25. e	30. x

Learning Objectives—Short Answer or Essay Questions—Answers

Learning Objective #1: Explain the meaning of the term *production* or *operations*.
Production (or *operations*) refers to the processes and activities for transforming resources into finished services and goods for customers. Resources include knowledge, physical materials, equipment, and labor that are systematically combined in a production facility to create *utility* for customers.

Learning Objective #2: Describe the three kinds of utility that operations processes provide for adding customer value.
Production provides businesses with economic results and it adds customer value by providing *utility*—the ability of a product to satisfy a want or need—in terms of form, time, and place:
• Form utility—By converting raw materials and human skills into finished goods and services, production creates form utility.
• Time utility —When a company makes products available when consumers want them.
• Place utility —When a company makes products available where they are convenient for consumers.

Learning Objective #3: Explain how companies with different business strategies are best served by having different operations capabilities.
Production is a flexible activity that can be molded into many shapes to give different operations capabilities (production capabilities) for different purposes. Its design is best driven from above by the firm's larger business strategy. When firms adopt different strategies for winning customers, they should also adjust their operations capabilities— what production must do especially well—to match the strategy. The operations capability that is appropriate for a low-cost strategy, for example, is different than the kind of competence for a firm that chooses a dependability strategy. Accordingly, the operations characteristics—such as number and size of production facilities, employee

skills, and kinds of equipment—will be different for the two firms, resulting in different operations capabilities that better support their different purposes.

Learning Objective #4: Identify the major factors that are considered in operations planning.

Operations planning includes five major considerations: (1) Capacity planning considers current and future capacity requirements for meeting anticipated customer demand. The amount of a product that a company can produce under normal conditions is its capacity, and it depends on how many people it employs and the number and size of its facilities. (2) Location planning is crucial because a firm's location affects costs of production, ease of transporting, access to skilled workers, and convenient accessibility for customers. (3) Layout planning determines the spatial arrangement of machinery, equipment, and facilities and affects how efficiently a company can respond to customer demand. A process layout is effective for make-to-order production specializing in custom jobs. A product layout, such as assembly lines, is often used for large-volume make-to-stock production. (4) Quality planning begins when products are being designed and extends into production operations for ensuring that the desired performance and consistency are built into products. (5) Methods planning considers each production step and the specific methods for performing it. The purpose is to reduce waste and inefficiency by improving process flows.

Learning Objective #5: Discuss the information contained in four kinds of operations schedules—the master production schedule, detailed schedule, staff schedule, and project schedule.

Operations scheduling identifies times when specific production activities will occur. The *master production schedule*, the top-level schedule for upcoming production, shows how many of which products will be produced in each time period to meet upcoming customer demand. *Detailed schedules* take a shorter-range perspective by specifying daily work assignments with start and stop times for assigned jobs at each work station. *Staff schedules* identify who and how many employees will be working, and when, for each work shift. Finally, *project schedules* provide information for completing large-scale projects.

Learning Objective #6: Identify the activities involved in operations control.

Once plans and schedules have been drawn up, *operations control* requires managers to monitor performance by comparing results against those plans and schedules. If schedules or quality standards are not met, managers take corrective action. *Follow-up*— checking to ensure that decisions are being implemented—is an essential facet of operations control. *Materials management*—including supplier selection, purchasing, transportation, warehousing, and inventory control—facilitates the flow of materials. It may use lean production systems, such as *just-in-time operations*, for smooth production flows that avoid inefficiencies, comply with schedules, eliminate unnecessary inventories, and continuously improve production processes. *Quality control* means taking action to ensure that operations produce products that meet specific quality standards.

Learning Objective #7: Identify the activities and underlying objectives involved in total quality management.

Total quality management (TQM) is a customer-driven culture for offering products with characteristics that customers want. It includes all of the activities necessary for getting customer-satisfying goods and services into the marketplace and, internally, getting every job to give better service to internal customers. TQM begins with leadership and a desire for continuously improving both processes and products. It considers all aspects of a business, including customers, suppliers, and employees. The TQM culture fosters an attitude of quality ownership among employees and suppliers—the idea that quality belongs to each person who creates it while performing a job—so that quality improvement becomes a continuous way of life.

Learning Objective #8: Explain how a supply chain strategy differs from traditional strategies for coordinating operations among firms.

The supply chain strategy is based on the idea that members of the *supply chain*—the stream of all activities and companies that add value in creating a product—will gain competitive advantage by working together as a coordinated unit. In contrast, traditional strategies assume that companies are managed as individual firms, each acting in its own interest. By managing the entire chain—using *supply chain management*—companies can more closely coordinate activities throughout the chain. By sharing information, overall costs and inventories can be reduced, quality can be improved, overall flow through the system can be improved, and deliveries to customers can be faster.

Critical Thinking Questions—Answers

1. **Explain how managers use operations control.**

   Operations control requires managers to monitor performance by comparing results with detailed plans and schedules. If schedules or quality standards aren't met, managers can take corrective action.

2. **How do managers motivate employees throughout the company and its suppliers to achieve quality goals?**

   Leaders of the quality movement use various methods and resources to foster a quality focus—training, verbal encouragement, teamwork, and tying compensation to work quality.

Brain Teaser—Answer

How do managers go about designing operations systems?

In designing operations systems, managers must identify each production step and the specific methods for performing it. They can then reduce waste and inefficiency by examining procedures on a step-by-step basis—an approach called methods improvement.

Chapter 8
Employee Behavior and Motivation

Learning Objectives
After reading this chapter, you should be able to:

1. Identify and discuss the basic forms of behaviors that employees exhibit in organizations.
2. Describe the nature and importance of individual differences among employees.
3. Explain the meaning and importance of psychological contracts and the person-job fit in the workplace.
4. Identify and summarize the most important models and concepts of employee motivation.
5. Describe some of the strategies and techniques used by organizations to improve employee motivation.

True-False
Indicate whether the statement is generally true or false by placing a "T" or an "F" in the space provided. If it is a false statement, correct it so that it becomes a true statement.

_____ 1. All organizations face the basic challenge of managing psychological contracts.

_____ 2. The key to increasing worker morale and productivity is to demonstrate to employees that their individual needs are different than the needs of the organization.

_____ 3. Evidence suggests that job satisfaction and employee morale may directly affect a company's performance.

_____ 4. In Frederick Taylor's view (the scientific management approach), people are motivated almost exclusively by money.

_____ 5. According to the Hawthorne effect, workers will be more productive if they believe they are receiving less special attention from managers.

_____ 6. Theory X argues that people are naturally responsible, growth oriented, self-motivated, and interested in being productive.

_____ 7. In attempting to motivate employees, Theory Y would emphasize management authority, and Theory X would emphasize employee growth and self-direction.

_____ 8. The most basic needs, according to Maslow's hierarchy, are self-actualization needs.

_____ 9. In Maslow's hierarchy of needs, the need for esteem can be met through job security and pension plans.

_____ 10. Hygiene factors, such as working conditions, company policies, and job security, have a negative effect on motivation only if they are deficient.

_____ 11. Motivators such as achievement, recognition, and responsibility are related negatively to increases in productivity.

_____ 12. The expectancy theory of motivation argues that people are motivated to work toward rewards that they want and they believe they have a reasonable chance of obtaining.

_____ 13. The equity theory of motivation argues that people evaluate their treatment by employers relative to the treatment of others.

_____ 14. Reinforcement is used when a company pays piecework rewards.

_____ 15. Management by objectives is a set of procedures involving both managers and subordinates in setting goals and evaluating progress.

_____ 16. Goal setting is most effective as a means of increasing employee motivation when those goals are imposed from above.

_____ 17. Employee empowerment can be an effective motivational tool.

_____ 18. Job sharing is a method of increasing job satisfaction by allowing workers to adjust work schedules on a daily or weekly basis.

_____ 19. Job enrichment reduces specialization and makes work more meaningful by expanding each job's responsibilities.

_____ 20. Today's employees want rewards that are quite different from those valued by earlier generations.

_____ 21. Studies suggest that workers today are interested in flexible working hours.

_____ 22. The challenges that make motivating workers difficult stem from changes in the economy, the work force, and organizational cultures.

Multiple Choice

Circle the one best answer for each of the following questions.

1. Managers need to
   a. realize the importance of maintaining good relations with their employees.
   b. create a climate of openness and trust with their employees.
   c. realize that leadership, motivation, and communication are the major elements that contribute to good human relations.
   d. All of the above.

2. Which of the following statements is *true*?
   a. Morale is the overall attitude that employees have toward their workplace.
   b. Job satisfaction is the degree of enjoyment that people derive from performing their jobs.
   c. Some of the most profitable companies are those with the greatest job satisfaction and highest employee morale.
   d. All of the above.

3. Frederick Taylor
   a. developed *scientific management*, a management approach that seeks to improve employee efficiency through the scientific study of work.
   b. believed workers are primarily motivated by a need to be loved and to feel a sense of belonging.
   c. believed paying workers more would reduce productivity.
   d. All of the above.

4. According to Maslow's hierarchy of needs
   a. the higher levels of the hierarchy need to be satisfied before the lower-level needs can be addressed.
   b. the lowest level is self-actualization—the need to become everything one is capable of.
   c. the need for esteem relates to the feelings of self-worth and respect from others.
   d. the social needs are the most basic requirements for human life and are seldom strong motivators for modern wage earners.

5. Employers providing job security and pension plans would best fulfill which of the following needs of workers?
   a. Physiological needs
   b. Safety (or security) needs
   c. Social needs
   d. Esteem needs

6. Employers giving employees the opportunity to expand their skills and take on additional responsibility would help satisfy which needs of workers?
   a. Security (or safety) needs
   b. Social needs
   c. Self-actualization needs
   d. Esteem needs

7. The two-factor theory emphasizes which two factors?
   a. Hygiene factors and motivators   b. Social and physiological needs
   b. Money and job security   d. Job enrichment and job sharing

8. Theory X assumes
   a. employees are irresponsible.
   b. employees are not ambitious and dislike work.
   c. managers must use force, control, or threats to motivate workers.
   d. All of the above.

9. According to the two-factor theory
   a. management may lessen dissatisfaction by improving hygiene factors that
       concern employees, but such improvements won't influence satisfaction.
   b. management can help employees feel motivated by paying attention to
       motivators such as achievement, recognition, responsibility, and other
       personally rewarding factors.
   c. a skilled, well-paid employee may be motivated to perform better if motivators
       are supplied, but a young, insecure employee who earns low wages still needs
       the support of strong hygiene factors to reduce dissatisfaction before motivators
       can be effective.
   d. All of the above.

10. Which of the following is NOT associated with Theory Y?
    a. Employees like work.
    b. Employees are naturally committed to certain goals and are capable of
        creativity.
    c. Managers must use force, control, or threats to motivate workers.
    d. Employees seek out responsibility under the right circumstances.

11. Which of the following statements is *true*?
    a. The assumptions behind Theory X emphasize management authority.
    b. The assumptions behind Theory Y emphasize employee growth and self-
        direction.
    c. Managers who adopt the expectancy theory should focus on the job
        responsibilities workers strive for and establish realistic steps to allow workers
        to achieve their goals.
    d. All of the above.

12. Which of the following statements is *true*?
    a. Management by objectives occurs when managers dictate goals to subordinates
        and evaluate workers based on their ability to realize these goals.
    b. The equity theory of motivation argues that people evaluate their treatment by
        employers relative to the treatment of others.
    c. Allowing workers a voice in company policy usually reduces morale because it
        increases the responsibility of workers.
    d. Flextime programs are a method of increasing job satisfaction by designing a
        more satisfactory fit between workers and their jobs.

13. Companies are trying to motivate their workers more by
    a. allowing employees to set clear and challenging personal goals that support organizational goals.
    b. using reinforcement.
    c. offering job rotation programs.
    d. All of the above.

14. Job enrichment is
    a. a method of increasing job satisfaction by adding one or more motivating factors to job activities.
    b. a scheduling system in which employees are allowed certain options regarding time arrival and departure.
    c. slicing a few hours off everybody's workweek and cutting pay to minimize layoffs.
    d. splitting a single full-time job between two employees for their convenience.

15. Which of the following is NOT one of the "Big Five" personality traits?
    a. Emotionality
    b. Agreeableness
    c. Conscientiousness
    d. Introvertism

Match the Terms and Concepts with Their Definitions

a. psychological contract
b. absenteeism
c. job satisfaction
d. morale
e. motivation

f. classical theory of motivation
g. Hawthorne effect
h. Theory X

i. Theory Y

j. hierarchy of needs model
k. two-factor theory
l. expectancy theory
m. equity theory
n. positive reinforcement

o. management by objectives

p. participative management
q. job enrichment

r. job redesign

s. work sharing
t. flextime programs
u. telecommuting
v. attitudes
w. organizational commitment
x. turnover

y. person-job fit
z. organizational citizenship
aa. individual differences

_____ 1. A reward that follows desired behaviors.

_____ 2. A method of increasing job satisfaction by designing a more satisfactory fit between workers and their jobs.

_____ 3. A person's beliefs and feelings about specific ideas, situations, or people.

_____ 4. The theory of motivation holding that people are naturally responsible, growth oriented, self-motivated, and interested in being productive.

_____ 5. The theory of motivation holding that people are motivated to work toward rewards that they want and that they believe they have a reasonable chance of obtaining.

_____ 6. The degree of enjoyment that people derive from performing their jobs.

_____ 7. An individual's identification with the organization and its mission.

_____ 8. The method of increasing job satisfaction by giving employees a voice in the management of their jobs and the company.

_____ 9. The method of increasing job satisfaction by allowing workers to adjust work schedules on a daily or weekly basis.

_____ 10. The extent to which a person's contributions and the organization's inducements match one another.

_____ 11. When an employee does not show up for work.

_____ 12. Positive behaviors that do not directly contribute to the bottom line.

_____ 13. The theory holding that workers are motivated solely by money.

_____ 14. The theory of motivation holding that people evaluate their treatment by employers relative to the treatment of others.

_____ 15. The set of expectations held by an employee concerning what he or she will contribute to an organization (referred to as *contributions*) and what the organization will in return provide the employee (referred to as *inducements*).

_____ 16. Personal attributes that vary from one person to another.

_____ 17. The method of increasing job satisfaction by adding motivating factors to job activities.

_____ 18. A form of flextime that allows people to perform some or all of a job away from standard office settings.

_____ 19. The annual percentage of an organization's workforce that leaves and must be replaced.

_____ 20. The overall attitude that employees have toward their workplace.

_____ 21. The theory of motivation describing five levels of human needs and arguing that basic needs must be fulfilled before people work to satisfy higher-level needs.

_____ 22. The method of increasing job satisfaction by allowing two or more people to share a single full-time job.

_____ 23. The set of forces that cause people to behave in certain ways.

_____ 24. A set of procedures involving both managers and subordinates in setting goals and evaluating progress.

_____ 25. The theory of motivation holding that job satisfaction depends on two types of factors: hygiene and motivation.

_____ 26. The tendency for productivity to increase when workers believe they are receiving special attention from management.

_____ 27. The theory of motivation that people are naturally irresponsible and uncooperative.

Fill in the Missing Parts

Fill in the missing blocks or pieces of the puzzle.

Maslow's Hierarchy of Needs

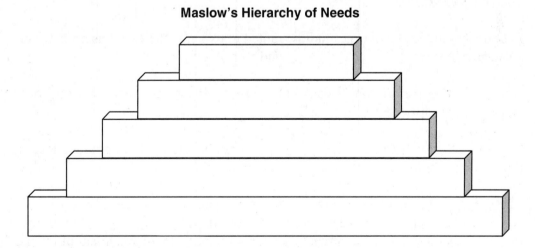

Herzberg's Two-Factor Theory

Hygiene Factors	Motivation Factors
1.	1.
2.	2.
3.	3.
4.	4.

McGregor's Theory X and Theory Y

Characteristics of a Theory X Manager	Characteristics of a Theory Y Manager
1.	1.
2.	2.
3.	3.
4.	4.

Fill in the Blanks

1. The percentage of a firm's workforce that leaves and must be replaced is _____.

2. Although job satisfaction and morale are important, employee _____ is even more critical to a firm's success.

3. Researchers in the Hawthorne studies wanted to examine the relationship between changes in the _____ and worker output.

4. A manager who locks a supply cabinet because he or she believes most of his or her employees are dishonest is likely a Theory _____ manager.

5. According to Herzberg's studies, _____ factors are likely to produce feelings that lie on a continuum from *dissatisfaction* to *no dissatisfaction*.

6. The _____ theory helps explain why some people do not work as hard as they can when their salaries are based purely on seniority. The _____ theory focuses on people evaluating their treatment by the firm relative to the treatment of others.

7. Combining tasks and establishing client relationships are ways to implement job _____.

8. When rewards are tied directly to performance, they serve as _____ reinforcement.

Learning Objectives—Short Answer or Essay Questions

Learning Objective #1: Identify and discuss the basic forms of behaviors that employees exhibit in organizations.

Learning Objective #2: Describe the nature and importance of individual differences among employees.

Learning Objective #3: Explain the meaning and importance of psychological contracts and the person-job fit in the workplace.

Learning Objective #4: Identify and summarize the most important models and concepts of employee motivation.

Learning Objective #5: Describe some of the strategies and techniques used by organizations to improve employee motivation.

Critical Thinking Questions

1. What is positive reinforcement, and how is it used by management?

2. Explain the concepts of participative management and empowerment.

Brain Teaser

What are the benefits of management by objectives (MBO) in collaborative goal setting?

ANSWERS

True-False—Answers

1. True
2. False: The key to increasing worker morale and productivity is to demonstrate to employees that their individual needs *coincide with* the needs of the organization.
3. True
4. True
5. False: According to the Hawthorne effect, workers will be more productive if they believe they are receiving *more* special attention from managers.
6. False: *Theory Y* argues that people are naturally responsible, growth oriented, self-motivated, and interested in being productive.
7. False: In attempting to motivate employees, *Theory X* would emphasize management authority, and *Theory Y* would emphasize employee growth and self-direction.
8. False: The most basic needs, according to Maslow's hierarchy, are *physiological* needs.
9. False: In Maslow's hierarchy of needs, the need for esteem can be met *by motivational techniques of recognition such as a job title*.
10. True
11. False: Motivators such as achievement, recognition, and responsibility are related *positively* to increases in productivity.
12. True
13. True
14. True
15. True
16. False: Goal setting is most effective as a means of increasing employee motivation when *employees have input into the creation of clear and challenging—but achievable—goals*.
17. True
18. False: *Flextime* is a method of increasing job satisfaction by allowing workers to adjust work schedules on a daily or weekly basis.
19. True
20. True
21. True
22. True

Multiple Choice—Answers

1. d	4. c	7. a	10. c	13. d
2. d	5. b	8. d	11. d	14. a
3. a	6. c	9. d	12. b	15. d

Match the Terms and Concepts with Their Definitions—Answers

1. n	6. c	11. b	16. aa	21. j	26. g
2. r	7. w	12. z	17. q	22. s	27. h
3. v	8. p	13. f	18. u	23. e	
4. i	9. t	14. m	19. x	24. o	
5. l	10. y	15. a	20. d	25. k	

Fill in the Missing Parts—Answers

1. Maslow's Hierarchy of Needs

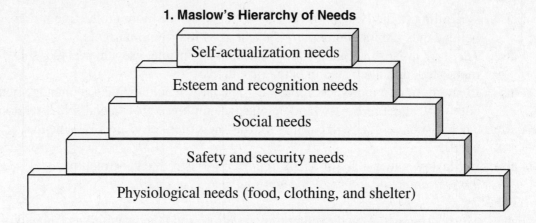

2. Herzberg's Two-Factor Theory

Hygiene Factors	Motivation Factors
1. Working conditions	1. Achievement
2. Company policies	2. Recognition
3. Job security	3. Responsibilities
4. Salaries, wages	4. Incentive pay

3. McGregor's Theory X and Theory Y

Theory X	Theory Y
1. People dislike work and will avoid it whenever possible	1. People like to work and consider it natural
2. Employees must be threatened by punishment to achieve goals	2. People naturally work towards goals they are committed to
3. Employees will avoid responsibility whenever possible	3. The average person can learn to accept responsibility
4. Employees value security above all other job factors	4. The average person's intellectual potential is only partially realized

Fill in the Blanks—Answers

1. turnover	4. X	7. redesign
2. motivation	5. hygiene	8. positive
3. physical environment	6. expectancy; equity	

Learning Objectives—Short Answer or Essay Questions—Answers

Learning Objective #1: Identify and discuss the basic forms of behaviors that employees exhibit in organizations.
Employee behavior is the pattern of actions by the members of an organization that directly or indirectly influences the organization's effectiveness. *Performance behaviors* are the total set of work-related behaviors that the organization expects employees to display. *Organizational citizenship* refers to the behavior of individuals who make a positive overall contribution to the organization. *Counterproductive behaviors* are those that detract from, rather than contribute to, organizational performance.

Learning Objective #2: Describe the nature and importance of individual differences among employees.
Individual differences are personal attributes that vary from one person to another. *Personality* is the relatively stable set of psychological attributes that distinguish one person from another. The *"big five" personality traits* are *agreeableness*, *conscientiousness*, *emotionality*, *extraversion*, and *openness*. *Emotional intelligence*, or *emotional quotient (EQ)*, refers to the extent to which people are self-aware, can manage their emotions, can motivate themselves, express empathy for others, and possess social skills. *Attitudes* reflect our beliefs and feelings about specific ideas, situations, or other people. Especially important attitudes are *job satisfaction* and *organizational commitment*.

Learning Objective #3: Explain the meaning and importance of psychological contracts and the person-job fit in the workplace.
A *psychological contract* is the overall set of expectations held by employees and the organization regarding what employees will contribute to the organization and what the organization will provide in return. A good *person-job fit* is achieved when the employee's contributions match the inducements the organization offers. Having a good match between people and their jobs can help enhance performance, job satisfaction, and motivation.

Learning Objective #4: Identify and summarize the most important models and concepts of employee motivation.
Motivation is the set of forces that cause people to behave in certain ways. Early approaches to motivation were based first on the assumption that people work only for money and then on the assumption that social needs are the primary way to motivate people. The *hierarchy of human needs model* holds that people at work try to satisfy one or more of five different needs. The *two-factor theory* argues that satisfaction and

dissatisfaction depend on hygiene factors, such as working conditions, and motivation factors, such as recognition for a job well done. *Expectancy theory* suggests that people are motivated to work toward rewards that they have a reasonable expectancy of obtaining. *Equity theory* focuses on social comparisons—people evaluating their treatment by the organization relative to the treatment of others.

Learning Objective #5: Describe some of the strategies and techniques used by organizations to improve employee motivation.
There are several major strategies and techniques often used to make jobs more interesting and rewarding. *Positive reinforcement* is used when a company or manager provides a reward when employees exhibit desired behaviors. *Punishment* is designed to change behavior by presenting people with unpleasant consequences if they exhibit undesired behaviors. *Management by objectives (MBO)* is a system of collaborative goal setting that extends from the top of an organization to the bottom. In *participative management and empowerment*, employees are given a voice in how they do their jobs and in how the company is managed. Using *teams* can also enhance motivation. *Job enrichment* adds motivating factors to job activities. *Job redesign* is a method of increasing job satisfaction by designing a more satisfactory fit between workers and their jobs. Some companies also use *modified work schedules*—different approaches to working hours. Common options include *work sharing (job sharing)*, *flextime programs*, and *telecommuting*.

Critical Thinking Questions—Answers

1. **What is positive reinforcement, and how is it used by management?**
   Positive reinforcement is used when a company or manager provides a reward when employees exhibit desired behaviors. When rewards are tied directly to performance, they serve as positive reinforcement.

2. **Explain the concepts of participative management and empowerment.**
   In participative management and empowerment, employees are given a voice in how they do their jobs and in how the company is managed—they become empowered to take greater responsibility for their own performance.

Brain Teaser—Answer

What are the benefits of management by objectives (MBO) in collaborative goal setting?

According to many experts, motivational impact is the biggest advantage of MBO. When employees sit down with managers to set upcoming goals, they learn more about companywide objectives, feel that they are an important part of a team, and see how they can improve companywide performance by reaching their own goals.

Chapter 9
Leadership and Decision Making

Learning Objectives
After reading this chapter, you should be able to:

1. Define *leadership* and distinguish it from management.
2. Summarize early approaches to the study of leadership.
3. Discuss the concept of situational approaches to leadership.
4. Describe transformational and charismatic perspectives on leadership.
5. Identify and discuss leadership substitutes and neutralizers.
6. Discuss leaders as coaches and examine gender and cross-cultural issues in leadership.
7. Describe strategic leadership, ethical leadership, and virtual leadership.
8. Relate leadership to decision making and discuss both rational and behavioral perspectives on decision making.

True-False
Indicate whether the statement is generally true or false by placing a "T" or an "F" in the space provided. If it is a false statement, correct it so that it becomes a true statement.

_____ 1. *Leadership* refers to the processes and behaviors used by someone, such as a manager, to motivate, inspire, and influence the behaviors of others.

_____ 2. All managers are leaders.

_____ 3. Organizations need both management and leadership if they are to be effective.

_____ 4. Management is necessary to achieve coordination and systematic results and to handle administrative activities during times of stability and predictability.

_____ 5. Biological factors were once considered a factor in the trait approach to leadership.

_____ 6. After looking at actual leadership behaviors, researchers focused on the trait approach to leadership.

_____ 7. The situational approach to leadership assumes that appropriate leader behavior varies from one situation to another.

_____ 8. The two primary approaches to leadership through the eyes of followers are transformational leadership and charismatic leadership.

_____ 9.   Transformational leadership focuses on the importance of leading during periods of stability.

_____ 10. Charismatic leadership is a type of influence based on the leader's personal charisma.

_____ 11. Those with ethical concerns about charismatic leadership believe those leaders may inspire blind faith in their followers, leading to inappropriate, unethical, or even illegal behaviors.

_____ 12. Leadership neutralizers are individual, task, and organizational characteristics that tend to outweigh the need for a leader to initiate or direct employee performance.

_____ 13. Individual ability, experience, training, knowledge, motivation, and professional orientation are among the characteristics that may substitute for leadership.

_____ 14. Among the recent changes in leadership that managers should recognize is the decreasing role of leaders as coaches.

_____ 15. Research suggests that female leaders are much more nurturing and supportive than male leaders.

_____ 16. As workforces are becoming more diverse, cross-cultural factors are playing a growing role in organizations.

_____ 17. Strategic leadership is a leader's ability to understand the complexities of both the organization and its environment and to lead change in the organization so as to enhance its competitiveness.

_____ 18. While effective strategic leaders must have a thorough and complete understanding of the internal aspects of an organization including its history, its culture, its strengths, and its weaknesses, they do not really need to understand the organization's external environment.

_____ 19. With virtual leadership, leaders and their employees work together in the same physical location and engage in personal interactions on a regular basis.

_____ 20. The first step in rational decision making is recognizing that a decision is necessary.

_____ 21. The more important the decision, the more attention is directed to developing alternatives.

Multiple Choice

Circle the best answer for each of the following questions.

1. Leadership is NOT closely associated with which of the following?
    a. Motivating
    b. Inspiring
    c. Influencing
    d. Controlling

2. Leadership is necessary to
    a. create change.
    b. direct change.
    c. help the organization get through tough times..
    d. All of the above.

3. Researchers focus on identifying essential leadership traits in which of the following?
    a. The trait approach to leadership
    b. The behavioral approach to leadership
    c. The task-focused leader behavior
    d. The employee-focused leader behavior

4. Which of the following is *true* regarding transformational leadership?
    a. It focuses on the importance of leading for change.
    b. Some leaders are able to adopt either transformational or transactional perspectives, depending on their circumstances.
    c. Occasionally leaders engage in transformational leadership to initiate and manage major change, such as managing a merger, creating a new work team, or redefining the organization's culture.
    d. All of the above.

5. A charismatic leader is less likely to have
    a. a lot of self-confidence.   b. a passive personality.
    c. confidence in their beliefs and ideals.   d. a need to influence people.

6. Which of the following is a leader's ability to understand the complexities of both the organization and its environment and to lead change in the organization so as to enhance its competitiveness?
    a. Charisma   b. Coaching
    c. Strategic leadership   d. Ethical leadership

7. In the rational decision-making process, implementing the chosen alternative involves
    a. implementation that may be easy or difficult.
    b. a chance of unanticipated consequences.
    c. considering employee resistance to change.
    d. All of the above.

8. Which of the following refers to an informal alliance of individuals or groups formed to achieve a common goal?
   a. Cartel
   b. Collectivism
   c. Coalition
   d. Strategic leadership

9. Which of the following came first?
   a. The trait approach to leadership
   b. The behavioral approach to leadership
   c. The situational approach to leadership
   d. Transformational leadership

10. Which of the following is NOT a leadership characteristic?
    a. The manager's value system
    b. Personal inclinations
    c. Feelings of insecurity
    d. Confidence in subordinates

11. Which of the following statements is *true*?
    a. Charismatic leaders are able to envision likely future trends and patterns, to set high expectations for themselves and for others, and to behave in ways that meet or exceed those expectations.
    b. Charismatic leaders are able to energize others by demonstrating personal excitement, personal confidence, and consistent patterns of success.
    c. Charismatic leaders enable others by supporting them, empathizing with them, and expressing confidence in them.
    d. All of the above.

12. Which of the following statements is *true*?
    a. Management by objectives occurs when managers dictate goals to subordinates and evaluate workers based on their ability to realize these goals.
    b. The equity theory of motivation argues that people evaluate their treatment by employers relative to the treatment of others.
    c. Allowing workers a voice in company policy usually reduces morale because it increases the responsibility of workers.
    d. Flextime programs are a method of increasing job satisfaction by designing a more satisfactory fit between workers and their jobs.

13. Companies are trying to motivate their workers more by
    a. allowing employees to set clear and challenging personal goals that support organizational goals.
    b. using reinforcement.
    c. offering job rotation programs.
    d. All of the above.

14. Job enrichment
    a. is a method of increasing job satisfaction by adding one or more motivating factors to job activities.
    b. is a scheduling system in which employees are allowed certain options regarding time arrival and departure.
    c. involves slicing a few hours off everybody's workweek and cutting pay to minimize layoffs.
    d. involves splitting a single full-time job between two employees for their convenience.

15. The management style in which managers generally issue orders and expect them to be obeyed without question is the
    a. autocratic management style of leadership.
    b. democratic management style of leadership.
    c. free-rein management style of leadership.
    d. oligarchic management style of leadership.

16. Leadership styles in the future will most likely move in the direction of
    a. a less autocratic approach to decision-making.
    b. a greater awareness of diversity in the workforce.
    c. a more "network" mentality rather than a "hierarchical" one.
    d. All of the above.

Match the Terms and Concepts with Their Definitions

a. behavioral approach to leadership
b. charismatic leadership
c. coalition
d. decision making

e. ethical leadership
f. intuition

g. leadership

h. leadership neutralizers

i. leadership substitutes

j. employee-focused leader behavior
k. risk propensity
l. strategic leadership
m. task-focused leader behavior

n. trait approach to leadership
o. transactional leadership

p. transformational leadership

q. virtual leadership

r. early leadership approaches

s. escalation of commitment
t. coach
u. collectivism
v. situational approach to leadership
w. individualism
x. first step in rational decision making
y. second step in rational decision making

z. third step in decision-making process

aa. fifth step in decision-making process

_____ 1.   Focused on identifying the essential traits that distinguished leaders.

_____ 2. The study of these began only about a century ago.

_____ 3. This step involves evaluating each of the alternatives.

_____ 4. The individual, task, and organizational characteristics that tend to outweigh the need for a leader to initiate or direct employee performance.

_____ 5. A leader's ability to understand the complexities of both the organization and its environment, and to lead change in the organization so as to enhance its competitiveness.

_____ 6. An informal alliance of individuals or groups formed to achieve a common goal.

_____ 7. Recognizing that a decision is necessary.

_____ 8. The set of abilities that allows a leader to recognize the need for change, to create a vision to guide that change, and to execute the change effectively.

_____ 9. This leader selects team members, provides general direction, trains and develops the team, and helps the team get the information and resources it needs.

_____ 10. Assumes that appropriate leader behavior varies from one situation to another.

_____ 11. The type of influence based on the leader's personal charisma.

_____ 12. Identify alternative courses of effective action.

_____ 13. An innate belief about something, often without conscious consideration.

_____ 14. A leader behavior focusing on how tasks should be performed in order to meet certain goals and to achieve certain performance standards.

_____ 15. Focused on determining what behaviors are employed by leaders.

_____ 16. Implementing the chosen alternative.

_____ 17. Leadership in settings where leaders and followers interact electronically rather than in face-to-face settings.

_____ 18. The leadership style found in Japan and characterized by emphasizing the group rather than the individual.

_____ 19. The leadership style found in the United States and characterized by emphasizing the individual rather than the group.

_____ 20. Choosing one alternative from among several options.

_____ 21. The leader behavior focusing on satisfaction, motivation, and well-being of employees.

_____ 22. The condition in which a decision maker becomes so committed to a course of action that he or she stays with it even when it appears to have been wrong.

_____ 23. The leader behaviors that reflect high ethical standards.

_____ 24. Comparable to management, it involves routine, regimented activities.

_____ 25. The extent to which a decision maker is willing to gamble when making a decision.

_____ 26. The processes and behaviors used by someone, such as a manager, to motivate, inspire, and influence the behaviors of others.

_____ 27. The factors that may render leader behaviors ineffective.

Fill in the Blanks

1. _____ is the processes and behaviors used by someone, such as a manager, to motivate, inspire, and influence the behaviors of others.

2. With the _____ approach to leadership, researchers focused on identifying the essential leadership traits, including intelligence, dominance, self-confidence, energy, activity, and knowledge about the job.

3. _____ leader behavior refers to when a leader focuses on the satisfaction, motivation, and well-being of his or her employees.

4. The _____ approach to leadership assumes that appropriate leader behavior varies from one situation to another.

5. _____ leadership is the set of abilities that allows a leader to recognize the need for change, to create a vision to guide that change, and to execute the change effectively.

6. Leadership _____ are individual, task, and organizational characteristics that tend to outweigh the need for a leader to initiate or direct employee performance.

7. Explicit plans and goals, rules and procedures, cohesive work groups, a rigid reward structure, and physical distance between supervisor and subordinate are organizational characteristics that may substitute for _____.

8. _____ leadership is a leader's ability to understand the complexities of both the organization and its environment and to lead change in the organization so as to enhance its competitiveness.

Learning Objectives—Short Answer or Essay Questions

Learning Objective #1: Define leadership and distinguish it from management.

Learning Objective #2: Summarize early approaches to the study of leadership.

Learning Objective #3: Discuss the concept of situational approaches to leadership.

Learning Objective #4: Describe transformational and charismatic perspectives on leadership.

Learning Objective #5: Identify and discuss leadership substitutes and neutralizers.

Learning Objective #6: Discuss leaders as coaches and examine gender and cross-cultural issues in leadership.

Learning Objective #7: Describe strategic leadership, ethical leadership, and virtual leadership.

Learning Objective #8: Relate leadership to decision making and discuss both rational and behavioral perspectives on decision making.

Critical Thinking Question

Describe the primary focus of transformational leadership.

ANSWERS

True-False—Answers

1. True
2. False: Leadership and management are different concepts.
3. True
4. True
5. True
6. False: In the late 1940s, most researchers began to shift away from the trait approach and to look at leadership as a set of actual behaviors.
7. True
8. True
9. False: Transformational leadership focuses on the importance of leading during periods of *change*.
10. True
11. True
12. False: Leadership *substitutes* are individual, task, and organizational characteristics that tend to outweigh the need for a leader to initiate or direct employee performance.
13. True
14. False: Among the recent changes in leadership that managers should recognize is the *increasing* role of leaders as coaches.
15. False: Research suggests that female leaders are *not necessarily more* nurturing and supportive than male leaders.
16. True
17. True
18. False: Effective strategic leaders must have a thorough and complete understanding of the internal aspects of an organization including its history, its culture, its strengths, and its weaknesses, *as well as* a grasp of the organization's external environment.
19. False: With virtual leadership, leaders and their employees may *work in locations that are far from one another, using arrangements such as telecommuting.*
20. True
21. True

Multiple Choice—Answers

1. d	4. d	7. d	10. c	13. d	16. d
2. d	5. b	8. c	11. d	14. a	
3. a	6. c	9. a	12. b	15. a	

Match the Terms and Concepts with Their Definitions—Answers

1. n	6. c	11. b	16. aa	21. j	26. g
2. r	7. x	12. y	17. q	22. s	27. h
3. z	8. p	13. f	18. u	23. e	
4. i	9. t	14. m	19. w	24. o	
5. l	10. v	15. a	20. d	25. k	

Fill in the Blanks—Answers

1. leadership   4. situational   7. leadership
2. trait   5. transformational   8 strategic
3. employee-focused   6. substitutes

Learning Objectives—Short Answer or Essay Questions—Answers

Learning Objective #1: Define *leadership* and distinguish it from management.
Leadership refers to the processes and behaviors used by someone to motivate, inspire, and influence the behaviors of others. While leadership and management are often related, they are not the same thing. A person can be a leader, a manager, both, or neither. Leadership involves such things as developing a vision, communicating that vision, energizing people, and directing change. Management, meanwhile, focuses more on outlining procedures, creating structure, monitoring results, and working toward tangible outcomes.

Learning Objective #2: Summarize early approaches to the study of leadership.
The *trait approach to leadership* focused on identifying the essential traits of successful leaders. The earliest researchers believed that important leadership traits included intelligence, dominance, self-confidence, energy, activity (versus passivity), and knowledge about the job. More recent researchers have started to focus on traits such as emotional intelligence, mental intelligence, drive, motivation, honesty and integrity, self-confidence, knowledge of the business, and charisma. While traits may play a role, however, their relevance has not been firmly established. The *behavioral approach* identified two basic and common leader behaviors: *task-focused* and *employee-focused* behaviors.

Learning Objective #3: Discuss the concept of situational approaches to leadership.
The *situational approach to leadership* proposes that there is no single best approach to leadership. Instead, a variety of situational factors influence the style or approach to leadership that is likely to be most effective. This approach was first proposed as a continuum of leadership behavior, ranging from the one extreme of having the leader make decisions alone to the other extreme of having employees make decisions with only minimal guidance from the leader. Each point on the continuum is influenced by characteristics of the leader, his or her subordinates, and the situation.

Learning Objective #4: Describe transformational and charismatic perspectives on leadership.

Transformational leadership (as distinguished from *transactional leadership*) focuses on the importance of leading for change. It can be defined as the set of abilities that allows a leader to recognize the need for change, to create a vision to guide that change, and to execute the change effectively. *Charismatic leadership* is a type of influence based on the leader's personal *charisma* (a form of interpersonal attraction that inspires support and acceptance). The basic concept of charisma suggests that charismatic leaders are likely to have a lot of self-confidence, confidence in their beliefs and ideals, and a strong need to influence people. They also tend to communicate high expectations about follower performance and to express confidence in their followers.

Learning Objective #5: Identify and discuss leadership substitutes and neutralizers.

Leadership substitutes are individual, task, and organizational factors that tend to outweigh the need for a leader to initiate or direct employee performance. In other words, if certain factors are present, the employee will perform his or her job capably, without the direction of a leader. Even if a leader is present and attempts to engage in various leadership behaviors, there also exist various *leadership neutralizers* that may render the leader's efforts ineffective. Such neutralizers include group factors (such as degree of group cohesiveness) as well as elements of the job itself that limit a leader's ability to lead.

Learning Objective #6: Discuss leaders as coaches and examine gender and cross-cultural issues in leadership.

Many organizations today are expecting their leaders to play more of a role of coach—to select team members, provide general direction, train and develop, and provide information but otherwise maintain a low profile and allow the group to function autonomously. Another factor that is clearly altering the face of leadership is the growing number of women advancing to higher levels in organizations. While there appear to be few differences between men and women leaders, the growing number of women leaders suggests a need for more study. Another changing perspective on leadership relates to cross-cultural issues. In this context, culture is used as a broad concept to encompass both international differences and diversity-based differences within one culture.

Learning Objective #7: Describe strategic leadership, ethical leadership, and virtual leadership.

Strategic leadership is the leader's ability to understand the complexities of both the organization and its environment and to lead change in the organization so as to enhance its competitiveness. Business leaders are also being called on to practice *ethical leadership*—that is, to maintain high ethical standards for their own conduct, to unfailingly exhibit ethical behavior, and to hold others in their organizations to the same standards. As more leaders and employees work in different settings, a better understanding of *virtual leadership* is also becoming more important. This includes understanding how leaders can best operate when they are located far from their subordinates.

Learning Objective #8: Relate leadership to decision making and discuss both rational and behavioral perspectives on decision making.

Decision making—choosing one alternative from among several options—is a critical management and leadership skill. The rational perspective prescribes a logical and orderly process for making decisions. It involves six steps: (1) recognizing and defining the decision situation, (2) identifying alternatives, (3) evaluating alternatives, (4) selecting the best alternative, (5) implementing the chosen alternative, and (6) following up and evaluating the results. The behavioral perspective acknowledges that things like political forces, intuition, escalation of commitment, and risk propensity are also important aspects of decision-making.

Critical Thinking Question—Answer

Describe the primary focus of transformational leadership.

Transformational leadership focuses on the importance of leading for change (as opposed to leading during a period of stability). Thus, transformational leadership is the set of abilities that allow a leader to recognize the need for change, to create a vision to guide that change, and to execute the change effectively. Some experts believe that change is such a vital organizational function that even successful firms need to change regularly to avoid becoming complacent and stagnant.

Chapter 10
Human Resource Management and Labor Relations

Learning Objectives
After reading this chapter, you should be able to:

1. Define *human resource management* and explain how managers plan for their organization's human resource needs.
2. Identify the tasks in *staffing* a company and discuss ways in which managers select, develop, and appraise employee performance.
3. Describe the main components of a compensation system and describe some of the key legal issues involved in hiring, compensating, and managing workers in today's workplace.
4. Discuss workforce diversity, the management of knowledge workers, and the use of a contingent workforce as important changes in the contemporary workplace.
5. Explain why workers organize into labor unions and describe the collective bargaining process.

True-False
Indicate whether the statement is generally true or false by placing a "T" or an "F" in the space provided. If it is a false statement, correct it so that it becomes a true statement.

_____ 1. Human resource management is the set of organizational activities directed at attracting, developing, and maintaining an effective workforce.

_____ 2. Human resource management has become a major challenge for businesses.

_____ 3. The first step in staffing business organizations is to train and develop employees.

_____ 4. After job analysis has been completed, the human resources manager develops a job description, and then a job specification.

_____ 5. The first stage in the hiring process is to interview each candidate for the job.

_____ 6. Interviewing is the session or procedure for orienting a new employee to the organization.

_____ 7. The most common method of work-based training is on-the-job training.

_____ 8. Many companies have developed performance appraisal systems to try to objectively evaluate employees according to set criteria.

_____ 9. Two methods of appraising performance of employees are the ranking and rating methods.

_____ 10. Basic compensation refers to the level of benefits provided to an employee.

_____ 11. Two general methods for compensating employees are through wages and salaries.

_____ 12. Wages (for hourly employees) and salaries (for non-hourly employees) are the most typical components of employee pay.

_____ 13. When an employee receives a "raise," it is an example of being compensated through a merit pay plan.

_____ 14. A commission is a group-based incentive system for distributing a portion of the company's profits to employees.

_____ 15. A benefit plan that allows an employee to choose from a variety of alternative benefits is called worker's compensation insurance.

_____ 16. The most popular types of benefits are health and retirement benefits.

_____ 17. The Equal Pay Act is a federal law forbidding discrimination on the basis of race, color, religious beliefs, sex, or national origin.

_____ 18. The practice of recruiting qualified employees belonging to racial, gender, or ethnic groups who are underrepresented in an organization is called the Fair Labor Standards Plan.

_____ 19. Sexual harassment is the practice or instance of making unwelcome sexual advances in the workplace.

_____ 20. Businesses are realizing that workforce diversity reduces their competitive advantage.

_____ 21. In recent years, the number of contingent workers employed has fallen dramatically.

_____ 22. A strike occurs when workers perform jobs at a slower pace than normal.

_____ 23. A boycott occurs when workers publicize their grievances at the entrance to an employer's facility.

_____ 24. If workers walk off their jobs, management can legally replace them with strikebreakers.

_____ 25. Not all strikes are legal.

_____ 26. Sympathy strikes are also known as secondary strikes.

_____ 27. Voluntary arbitration is a method of resolving a labor dispute in which both parties are legally required to accept the judgment of a neutral party.

_____ 28. Arbitration is always legally required to settle bargaining disputes.

Multiple Choice
Circle the best answer for each of the following questions.

1. Which of the following is NOT one of the functions of human resource management?
    a. Recruiting new employees
    b. Training and developing employees
    c. Managing employees
    d. Appraising and compensating employees

2. Which of the following statements is *true*?
    a. Keeping track of the labor market is quite easy.
    b. Effective human resource management is becoming more important in business.
    c. External recruiting is almost always more preferable to selecting a candidate to fill a position internally.
    d. The part-time labor force has shrunk in recent years.

3. Job analysis requires the human resource manager to
    a. develop a job description followed by a job specification.
    b. develop a job specification followed by a job description.
    c. continue to the next step, which is to determine future human resource needs.
    d. continue to the next step, which is to select an employee from a pool of candidates.

4. Which of the following correctly describes the steps involved in the human resource planning process?
    a. Develop a plan to match labor demand and supply, forecast internal and external supply of labor, forecast demand for labor, and then determine the job analysis.
    b. Develop a plan to match labor demand and supply, forecast internal and external supply of labor, determine the job analysis, and then forecast demand for labor.
    c. Determine the job analysis, forecast demand for labor, forecast internal and external supply of labor, and then develop a plan to match labor demand and supply.
    d. Forecast internal and external supply of labor, develop a plan to match labor demand and supply, determine the job analysis, and then forecast demand for labor.

5. Which of the following statements is *true*?
   a. When managers have determined that new employees are needed, they must then turn their attention to recruiting and hiring the right mix of people.
   b. Both internal and external staffing starts with effective recruiting.
   c. Once the recruiting process has attracted a pool of applicants, the next step is to select someone to hire.
   d. All of the above.

6. Which of the following would NOT be appropriate to ask a candidate during an interview?
   a. Why do you wish to change employment?
   b. What are your expectations of this position?
   c. What is your religious affiliation?
   d. What are your long-term goals?

7. Which of the following ties training and development activities to task performance?
   a. An orientation program
   b. A work-based program
   c. An instructional-based program
   d. A management-development program

8. Which of the following is *true*?
   a. A growing number of companies are helping their employees while they help themselves by offering college degree programs.
   b. The biggest problem with appraisal systems is finding a way to measure performance.
   c. Two general ways employees are compensated is though wages and salaries, and through benefits.
   d. All of the above.

9. Performance appraisals
   a. are the specific and formal evaluations of employees in order to determine the degree to which the employees are performing effectively.
   b. are important because they provide a benchmark to better assess the extent to which recruiting and selection processes are adequate.
   c. help managers assess the extent to which they are recruiting and selecting the best employees.
   d. All of the above.

10. Which of the following is *false* concerning compensation?
    a. Hourly employees earn wages; non-hourly employees earn salaries.
    b. Comparable worth is a concept of equal pay for jobs that are equal in value to the organization and require similar levels of education, training, and skills.
    c. Profit-sharing is a payment to an employee equal to a certain percentage of sales made by that employee.
    d. A piece-rate incentive plan provides payment for each unit produced.

11. Accepting a lower base pay in exchange for bonuses based on meeting production or other goals is
    a. knowledge-based pay.
    b. performance-based compensation.
    c. a sales commission.
    d. a comparable worth pay scheme.

12. A company-sponsored program for providing retirees with income is
    a. a private pension plan.
    b. a stock option plan.
    c. an employee stock-ownership plan.
    d. a merit-pay plan.

13. Which of the following statements is *true*?
    a. A cafeteria benefits plan allows employees to choose the unique combination of benefits that suit their needs.
    b. Social security and worker's compensation are mandated plans offered to all employees.
    c. Although no U.S. laws mandate paid time off, it is now expected by most employees.
    d. All of the above.

14. Which of the following plans is NOT available to all employees in a firm?
    a. Profit-sharing
    b. Merit pay increases
    c. Pay-for-knowledge plans
    d. Profit-sharing

15. Which of the following statements is *true*?
    a. Comparable worth is the principle that jobs worth the same should be compensated at the same level regardless of who performs them.
    b. An affirmative action plan is a federal law requiring employees to provide unpaid leave for specific family and medical reasons.
    c. The Civil Rights Act establishes minimum wage and overtime pay requirements.
    d. In recent years the number of contingent workers has decreased dramatically.

16. Which of the following is an option for labor in the event that negotiations with management break down?
    a. Employ strikebreakers
    b. Institute a lockout
    c. Impose a boycott
    d. Fire all strikers

17. Which of the following is an option for management in the event that negotiations with labor break down?
    a. Go on strike
    b. Mediation and Arbitration
    c. Impose a slowdown
    d. Implement a boycott

18. Which of the following is true concerning labor-management relations?
    a. Employees and managers are becoming more cooperative and less adversarial.
    b. To enhance labor-management relations, management could offer better pay and
        working conditions, establish grievance procedures, comply with legislation that
        protects employee rights, and involve workers in the operation of the business.
    c. To enhance labor-management relations, labor could help management find
        ways to cut costs, accept more flexible compensation packages, and reduce
        cumbersome work rules.
    d. All of the above.

19. Compulsory arbitration is a method of resolving a labor dispute in which
    a. a third party suggests a settlement.
    b. workers are denied access to the employer's workplace.
    c. both parties agree to submit to the judgment of a neutral party.
    d. both parties are legally required to accept the judgment of a neutral party.

20. Which of the following statements is *true*?
    a. When union members strike, companies have no recourse except to accept it.
    b. An employer may permanently replace workers who strike because of unfair
        practices.
    c. Labor and management can call in mediators or arbitrators to help settle their
        disputes.
    d. In mediation, the mediator's decision is legally binding.

Match the Terms and Concepts with Their Definitions

a. human resource management	r. strike	ii. equal employment opportunity
b. job analysis	s. collective bargaining	jj. illegal discrimination
c. job description	t. bonus	kk. protected class
d. job specification	u. wages	ll. equal employment opportunity commission (EEOC)
e. replacement chart	v. salary	mm. compensation system
f. employee information system (skills inventory)	w. work slowdown	nn. strike breaker
g. recruiting	x. lockout	oo. boycott
h. internal recruiting	y. merit salary system	pp. picketing
i. external recruiting	z. pay-for-knowledge plan	qq. mediation
j. off-the-job training	aa. arbitration	rr. Occupational Safety and Health Act of 1970
k. compulsory arbitration	bb. incentive program	ss. sexual harassment
l. on-the-job training	cc. gainsharing plan	tt. quid pro quo harassment

m. vestibule training

n. labor relations

o. performance appraisal

p. cost of living adjustment

q. wage reopener clause

dd. profit-sharing plan

ee. benefits

ff. worker's compensation insurance

gg. labor union

hh. cafeteria benefit plan

uu. hostile work environment

vv. employment at will

ww. workforce diversity

xx. knowledge worker

yy. contingent worker

_____ 1.   The process of dealing with employees who are represented by a union.

_____ 2.   Compensation in the form of money paid for discharging the responsibilities of a job.

_____ 3.   The method of resolving a labor dispute in which a third party suggests, but does not impose, a settlement.

_____ 4.   Labor action in which workers refuse to buy the products of a targeted employer.

_____ 5.   A computerized system containing information on each employee's education, skills, work experiences, and career aspirations.

_____ 6.   A group of individuals working together to achieve shared job-related goals, such as higher pay, shorter working hours, more job security, greater benefits, or better working conditions.

_____ 7.   The method of resolving a labor dispute in which both parties are legally required to accept the judgment of a neutral party.

_____ 8.   A set of individuals who, by nature of one or more common characteristics, are protected by law from discrimination on the basis of any of those characteristics.

_____ 9.   Labor action in which workers publicize their grievances at the entrance to an employer's facility.

_____ 10.   The range of workers' attitudes, values, and behaviors that differ by gender, race, and ethnicity.

_____ 11.   An incentive plan that rewards groups for productivity improvements.

_____ 12.   Labor action in which employees temporarily walk off the job and refuse to work.

_____ 13. Work-based training, sometimes informal, conducted while an employee is in an actual work situation.

_____ 14. A worker hired as a permanent or temporary replacement for a striking employee.

_____ 15. A formal evaluation of an employee's job performance in order to determine the degree to which the employee is performing effectively.

_____ 16. Compensation in the form of money paid for time worked.

_____ 17. An employee who is of value because of the knowledge that he or she possesses.

_____ 18. The method of resolving a labor dispute in which both parties agree to submit to the judgment of a neutral party.

_____ 19. The systematic evaluation of the duties, working conditions, tools, materials, and equipment related to the performance of a job.

_____ 20. A benefit plan that sets limits on benefits per employee, each of whom may choose from a variety of alternative benefits.

_____ 21. The federal agency enforcing several discrimination-related laws.

_____ 22. An individual performance incentive in the form of a special payment made over and above the employee's salary.

_____ 23. A worked-based training conducted in a simulated environment away from the work site.

_____ 24. The listing of each managerial position, who occupies it, how long that person will likely stay in the job, and who is qualified as a replacement.

_____ 25. A form of sexual harassment in which sexual favors are requested in return for job-related benefits.

_____ 26. An individual incentive linking compensation to performance in nonsales jobs.

_____ 27. The process by which labor and management negotiate conditions of employment and draft a labor contract for union-represented workers.

_____ 28. The systematic analysis of jobs in an organization.

_____ 29. Labor contract clause tying future raises to changes in consumer purchasing power.

_____ 30. The practice of attracting people outside an organization to apply for jobs.

_____ 31. Legally mandated nondiscrimination in employment on the basis of race, creed, sex, or national origin.

_____ 32. The process of attracting qualified persons to apply for open jobs.

_____ 33. An incentive plan for distributing bonuses to employees when company profits rise above a certain level.

_____ 34. The clause allowing wage rates to be renegotiated during the life of a labor contract.

_____ 35. The principle, increasingly modified by legislation and judicial decision, that organizations should be able to retain or dismiss employees at their discretion.

_____ 36. A set of organizational activities directed at attracting, developing, and maintaining an effective workforce.

_____ 37. The practice of considering present employees as candidates for job openings.

_____ 38. Legally required insurance covering workers who are injured or become ill on the job.

_____ 39. The federal law setting and enforcing guidelines for protecting workers from unsafe conditions and potential health hazards in the workplace.

_____ 40. The total package of rewards that organizations provide to individuals in return for their labor.

_____ 41. Training conducted in a controlled environment away from the work site.

_____ 42. Description of the skills, abilities, and other credentials required by a job.

_____ 43. Labor action in which workers perform jobs at a slower than normal pace.

_____ 44. A form of sexual harassment, deriving from off-color jokes, lewd comments, and so forth, that makes the work environment uncomfortable for some employees.

_____ 45. Discrimination among people that is not job related.

_____ 46. An employee hired on something other than a full-time basis to supplement an organization's permanent workforce.

_____ 47. A special compensation program designed to motivate high performance.

_____ 48. A management tactic whereby workers are denied access to the employer's workplace.

_____ 49. A practice or instance of making unwelcome sexual advances in the workplace.

_____ 50. An incentive plan to encourage employees to learn new skills or become proficient at different jobs.

_____ 51. Compensation other than wages and salaries.

Jeopardy

Complete the question to each of the following answers as quickly as you can.

Staffing	Selecting Staff	Incentives
Process of attracting qualified people What is _____?	Process of determining predictive value of data What is _____?	Links raises to performance levels in nonsales jobs What is a/n _____?
Consideration of present employees for openings What is _____?	Evaluations of skills, abilities, or aptitudes What are _____?	Where managers are rewarded for especially productive output What is _____?
Consideration of outside employees for openings What is _____?	Face-to-face evaluation of qualified candidates for a job What is a/n _____?	Profits earned above a certain level are distributed to employees What are _____?

Learning Objectives—Short Answer or Essay Questions

Learning Objective #1: Define *human resource management* and explain how managers plan for their organization's human resource needs.

Learning Objective #2: Identify the tasks in *staffing* a company and discuss ways in which organizations select, develop, and appraise employee performance.

Learning Objective #3: Describe the main components of a compensation system and describe some of the key legal issues involved in hiring, compensating, and managing workers in today's workplace.

Learning Objective #4: Discuss workforce diversity, the management of knowledge workers, and the use of a contingent workforce as important changes in the contemporary workplace.

Learning Objective #5: Explain why workers organize into labor unions and describe the collective bargaining process.

Critical Thinking Questions

1. Describe what it means to be a member of a protected class in the workplace.

2. Why is pay for performance (or variable pay) a widely used incentive program?

Brain Teaser

Explain the concept of employment at will.

ANSWERS

True-False—Answers

1. True
2. True
3. False: The first step in staffing business organizations is to *plan*, or to *forecast, future staffing needs*.
4. True
5. False: The first stage in the hiring process is to *select a small number of qualified candidates from all of the applications received*.
6. False: *Orientation* is the procedure for orienting a new employee to the organization.
7. True
8. True
9. True
10. False: Basic compensation refers to the *base* level of *wages or salary* paid to an employee.
11. False: Two general methods for compensating employees are through wages and salaries, *and through benefits (and services)*.
12. True
13. True
14. False: *Profit-sharing* is a group-based incentive system for distributing a portion of the company's profits to employees.
15. False: A benefit plan that allows an employee to choose from a variety of alternative benefits is called a *cafeteria benefit plan*.
16. True
17. False: The *Civil Rights Act of 1964* is a federal law forbidding discrimination on the basis of race, color, religious beliefs, sex, or national origin.
18. False: The practice of recruiting qualified employees who are underrepresented in an organization is called *an affirmative action plan*.
19. True
20. False: Businesses are realizing that diversity in their workforce *increases* their competitive advantage.
21. False: In recent years, the number of contingent workers employed has *risen* dramatically.
22. False: A *slowdown* occurs when workers perform jobs at a slower pace than normal.
23. False: *Picketing* occurs when workers publicize their grievances at the entrance to an employer's facility.
24. True
25. True
26. True
27. False: *Compulsory arbitration* is a method of resolving a labor dispute in which both parties are legally required to accept the judgment of a neutral party.
28. False: Arbitration is sometimes, but not always, legally required.

Multiple Choice—Answers

1. c	5. d	9. d	13. d	17. b
2. b	6. c	10. c	14. b	18. d
3. a	7. b	11. b	15. a	19. d
4. c	8. d	12. a	16. c	20. c

Match the Terms and Concepts with Their Definitions—Answers

1. n	9. pp	17. yy	24. e	31. ii	38. ff	45. jj
2. v	10. xx	18. aa	25. tt	32. g	39. rr	46. zz
3. qq	11. cc	19. c	26. y	33. dd	40. mm	47. bb
4. oo	12. r	20. hh	27. s	34. q	41. j	48. x
5. f	13. l	21. ll	28. b	35. vv	42. d	49. ss
6. gg	14. nn	22. t	29. p	36. a	43. w	50. z
7. k	15. o	23. m	30. i	37. h	44. uu	51. ee
8. kk	16. u					

Jeopardy—Answers

Staffing	Selecting Staff	Incentives
What is <u>recruiting</u>?	What is <u>validation</u>?	What is a <u>merit salary system</u>?
What is <u>internal recruiting</u>?	What are <u>tests</u>?	What is <u>variable pay</u>?
What is <u>outside recruiting</u>?	What is an <u>interview</u>?	What are <u>profit sharing plans</u>?

Learning Objectives—Short Answer or Essay Questions—Answers

Learning Objective #1: Define *human resource management* and explain how managers plan for their organization's human resource needs.
Human resource management is the set of organizational activities directed at attracting, developing, and maintaining an effective workforce. *Job analysis* is a systematic analysis of jobs within an organization resulting in two things: a *job description* and a *job specification*. Managers must plan for future needs by assessing past trends, future plans, and general economic trends. Forecasting labor supply is really two tasks: (a) forecasting internal supply and (b) forecasting external supply. The next step in HR planning is matching HR supply and demand. If a shortfall is predicted, new employees can be hired.

Learning Objective #2: Identify the tasks in staffing a company and discuss ways in which organizations select, develop, and appraise employee performance.
Staffing means recruiting and hiring the right mix of people. *Recruiting* involves attracting qualified persons to apply for open jobs, either from within the organization or from outside the organization. Recruiting methods include the Internet, advertising, campus interviews, employment agencies or executive search firms, and referrals. The next step is the selection process is the gathering of information that will predict applicants' job success and then hiring the most promising candidates. Selection techniques include application forms; tests of ability, aptitude, or knowledge; and interviews. New employees must be trained and allowed to develop job skills. *On-the-job training* occurs while the employee is at work. *Off-the-job training* takes place at off-site locations where controlled environments allow focused study. Some firms use *vestibule training*—off-the-job training in simulated work environments. In larger firms, *performance appraisals* show how well workers are doing their jobs.

Learning Objective #3: Describe the main components of a compensation system and describe some of the key legal issues involved in hiring, compensating, and managing workers in today's workplace.
A *compensation system* is the total package of rewards that a firm offers employees in return for their labor. Although *wages and salaries* are key parts of all compensation systems, most also include *incentives* and *employee benefits programs*. Beyond a certain point, money motivates employees only when tied directly to performance. One way to establish this link is the use of *incentive programs*—special pay programs designed to motivate high performance. *Benefits*—compensation other than wages and salaries—comprise a large percentage of most compensation budgets. The law requires most companies to provide social security retirement benefits and workers' compensation insurance. Companies may provide health, life, disability insurance, and retirement plans.

HR management is heavily influenced by the law. One area of HR regulation is *equal employment opportunity*. This regulation protects people from unfair or inappropriate discrimination in the workplace. Because illegal discrimination is based on a prejudice about classes of individuals, laws protect various classes. A *protected class* consists of all individuals who share one or more common characteristics as indicated by a given law (such as race, color, religion, gender, age, national origin, and so forth).

Learning Objective #4: Discuss workforce diversity, the management of knowledge workers, and the use of a contingent workforce as important changes in the contemporary workplace.
Workforce diversity refers to the range of workers' attitudes, values, beliefs, and behaviors that differ by gender, race, age, ethnicity, physical ability, and other relevant characteristics. Many U.S. organizations regard diversity as a competitive advantage. Employees who add value because of what they know are usually called *knowledge workers*, and managing them skillfully helps to determine which firms will be successful in the future. *Contingent workers*, including independent contractors, on-call workers, temporary employees, contract and leased employees, and part-time employees, work for organizations on something other than a permanent or full-time basis.

Learning Objective #5: Explain why workers organize into labor unions and describe the collective bargaining process.

A *labor union* is a group of individuals working together to achieve shared job-related goals. *Labor relations* refers to the process of dealing with employees represented by a union. The collective bargaining process begins when the union is recognized as the negotiator for its members. The bargaining cycle begins when union leaders and management meet to agree on a contract. When a compromise is reached, the agreement is voted on by union members.

An *impasse* occurs when management and labor fail to agree on a contract. Each side can use several tactics to support its cause until the impasse is resolved. An important union tactic is the *strike*, which occurs when employees temporarily walk off the job. Unions may also use *picketing*, in which workers demonstrate at an employer's facility. Under a *boycott*, union members agree not to buy products of a targeted employer. During a *work slowdown*, workers perform their jobs at a slower pace than normal. During a *sickout*, large numbers of workers call in sick. Management may resort to *lockouts,* denying employees access to the workplace. A firm can also hire *strikebreakers*, temporary or permanent replacements, but the law forbids the permanent replacement of workers who strike because of unfair practices.

Rather than use these tactics, labor and management can call in a third party to help resolve the dispute. Common options include *mediation*, *voluntary arbitration*, and *compulsory arbitration*.

Critical Thinking Questions—Answers

1. **Describe what it means to be a member of a protected class in the workplace.**
    To combat illegal discrimination, laws have been passed to protect various classes of individuals. A protected class consist of all individuals who share one or more common characteristics as indicated by a given law. The most common criteria for defining protected classes include race, color, religion, gender, age, national origin, disability status, and status as a military veteran.

2. **Why is pay for performance (or variable pay) a widely used incentive program?**
    Many firms say that variable pay is a better motivator than merit raises because the range between generous and mediocre merit raises is usually quite small.

Brain Teaser—Answer

Explain the concept of employment at will.

The concept of employment at will holds that both employer and employee have the mutual right to terminate an employment relationship at any time for any reason, with or without advanced notice to the one another.

Chapter 11
Marketing Processes and Consumer Behavior

Learning Objectives
After reading this chapter, you should be able to:

1. Explain the concept of marketing and identify the five forces that constitute the external marketing environment.
2. Explain the purpose of a marketing plan and identify the four components of the marketing mix.
3. Explain market segmentation and how it is used in target marketing.
4. Describe the key factors that influence the consumer buying process.
5. Discuss the three categories of organizational markets.
6. Explain the definition of a product as a value package and classify goods and services.
7. Describe the key considerations in the new product development process.
8. Explain the importance of branding and packaging.
9. Discuss the challenges that arise in adopting an international marketing mix.
10. Identify the ways that small businesses can benefit from an understanding of the marketing mix.

True-False
Indicate whether the statement is generally true or false by placing a "T" or an "F" in the space provided. If it is a false statement, correct it so that it becomes a true statement.

_____ 1. Marketing is a set of processes for creating, communicating, and delivering value to customers and for managing customer relationships in ways that benefit the organization and its stakeholders.

_____ 2. Firms that sell their products to other manufacturers engage in consumer marketing.

_____ 3. The political-legal environment of marketing includes the context within which people's values, beliefs, and ideas affect marketing decisions.

_____ 4. The technological environment of marketing consists of the conditions, such as inflation, recession, and interest rates, that influence consumer and organizational spending patterns.

_____ 5. The competitive environment of marketing is the environment in which marketers must persuade buyers to purchase their products rather than those of their competitors.

_____ 6. Brand competition is competitive marketing of domestic products against foreign products.

_____ 7. A substitute product is a product that is dissimilar to those of competitors but that can fulfill the same need.

_____ 8. Product features are the qualities that a company builds into a product.

_____ 9. Product differentiation is the creation of a product or product image that differs enough from existing products to attract consumers.

_____ 10. The components of the marketing mix are price, promotion, place, and personality.

_____ 11. Marketing begins with a promotion strategy.

_____ 12. In the marketing mix, "place" refers to distribution.

_____ 13. A target market is a group of people that have similar wants and needs and that can be expected to show interest in the same products.

_____ 14. Market segmentation is dividing a market into categories of customer types.

_____ 15. Market segmentation is designed to shut some customers out of the market.

_____ 16. Geographic segmentation is the classification of customers on the basis of their psychological makeup.

_____ 17. The categories of consumer products are convenience, shopping, and specialty goods.

_____ 18. When marketing internationally, managers must take into account different social, political, and economic environments found in foreign countries.

_____ 19. Branding is the process of using symbols to communicate the qualities of a product made by a particular producer.

_____ 20. When making buying decisions, consumers first determine or respond to a problem or a need and then collect as much information as they think is necessary before making a purchase.

_____ 21. Consumer markets are markets in which customers buy goods or services for resale or for use in conducting their own operations.

_____ 22. One important difference between consumer and organizational buying behavior is that organizational buyers are usually better informed in the buying decision.

Multiple Choice

Circle the best answer for each of the following questions.

1. Marketing involves
   a. selling a product.   b. selling services.
   c. selling ideas and causes.   d. All of the above.

2. Which of the following statements is correct?
   a. Marketing plans and strategies are influenced by the external environment.
   b. Consumer goods are products purchased by companies to produce other products.
   c. A marketing manager has a big influence on the external marketing environment.
   d. All of the above.

3. Competition marketing that appeals to consumer perceptions of similar products is
   a. substitute product competition.   b. brand competition.
   c. international competition.   d. impossible.

4. The external marketing environment that includes the laws and regulations, both domestic and foreign, that may define or constrain business activities is known as the
   a. economic environment.   b. sociocultural environment.
   c. political-legal environment.   d. technological environment.

5. The external marketing environment that includes the context within which people's values, beliefs, and ideas affect marketing decisions is known as the
   a. competitive environment.   b. sociocultural environment.
   c. political-legal environment.   d. technological environment.

6. When marketers try to persuade buyers to purchase their products rather than those of their competitors, they are focusing on the
   a. competitive environment.   b. sociocultural environment.
   c. economic environment.   d. technological environment.

7. Which of the following is NOT one of the four Ps of the marketing mix?
   a. Product   b. Place
   c. Promotion   d. Persistence

8. Distribution is that part of the marketing mix concerned with
   a. creating a product or product image that differs from existing products.
   b. selecting the most appropriate price at which to sell a product.
   c. getting products from producers to consumers.
   d. creating a good, service, or idea designed to fill a consumer need.

9. Which component of the marketing mix involves communicating information about a product?
   a. Promotion
   b. Product
   c. Place
   d. Price

10. Which component of the marketing mix involves decisions about the channels through which a product is made available to consumers?
   a. Promotion
   b. Product
   c. Place
   d. Price

11. Which component of the marketing mix involves the decision whether to undertake personal selling or to partake in public relations?
   a. Promotion
   b. Product
   c. Place
   d. Price

12. The practice of building long-term, satisfying relationships with customers and suppliers is
   a. customer marketing.
   b. database marketing.
   c. relationship marketing.
   d. one-to-one marketing.

13. When markets are segmented according to characteristics of populations, this is known as
   a. geographic segmentation.
   b. demographic segmentation.
   c. psychographic segmentation.
   d. product use segmentation.

14. Which of the following is a classification of industrial products?
   a. Capital items
   b. Convenience goods
   b. Shopping items
   d. Specialty goods

15. Organizational markets fall into which of the following three categories?
   a. Product, resource, and money markets
   b. Industrial, reseller, and government/institutional markets
   c. Primary, secondary, and post-secondary markets
   d. Goods, services, and technology/idea markets

16. A brand-name product for whose name the seller has purchased the right from an organization is known as a
   a. licensed brand.
   b. national brand.
   c. private brand.
   d. specialty brand.

17. Which of the following are factors that influence consumer behavior?
    a.   Culture and social class
    b.   Lifestyle and personality
    c.   Self-image
    d.   All of the above.

Match the Terms and Concepts with Their Definitions

a. marketing
b. consumer goods
c. industrial goods
d. services
e. relationship marketing
f. external environment
g. substitute product
h. brand competition
i. international competition
j. marketing mix
k. product
l. product differentiation

m. distribution
n. target market
o. market segmentation
p. geographic variables
q. demographic variables
r. psychographic variables
s. product line
t. consumer behavior
u. brand loyalty
v. rational motives
w. emotional motives
x. convenience good/service

y. shopping good/service
z. specialty good/service
aa. expense item
bb. capital item
cc. product mix
dd. speed to market
ee. branding
ff. industrial market
gg. reseller market
hh. institutional market
ii. national brand
jj. packaging

_____ 1.   The reasons for purchasing a product that are based on nonobjective factors.

_____ 2.   Expensive, long-lasting, infrequently purchased industrial product such as a building.

_____ 3.   Consumer characteristics, such as lifestyles, opinions, interests, and attitudes, that may be considered in developing a segmentation strategy.

_____ 4.   A set of processes for creating, communicating, and delivering value to customers and for managing customer relationships in ways that benefit the organization and its stakeholders.

_____ 5.   Competitive marketing that appeals to consumer perceptions of similar products.

_____ 6.   The marketing strategy that emphasizes lasting relationships with customers and suppliers.

_____ 7.   Geographical units that may be considered in developing a segmentation strategy.

_____ 8.   An organizational market consisting of intermediaries who buy and resell finished goods.

_____ 9. A moderately expensive, infrequently purchased product.

_____ 10. A brand-name product produced by, widely distributed by, and carrying the name of a manufacturer.

_____ 11. The creation of a product or product image that differs enough from existing products to attract consumers.

_____ 12. The products purchased by companies to produce other products.

_____ 13. The various facets of the decision process by which customers come to purchase and consume products.

_____ 14. The characteristics of populations that may be considered in developing a segmentation strategy.

_____ 15. The combination of product, pricing, promotion, and distribution strategies used to market products.

_____ 16. A group of people that has similar wants and needs and that can be expected to show interest in the same products.

_____ 17. The process of using symbols to communicate the qualities of a product made by a particular producer.

_____ 18. An inexpensive product purchased and consumed rapidly and regularly.

_____ 19. The products purchased by consumers for personal use.

_____ 20. The part of the marketing mix concerned with getting products from producers to consumers.

_____ 21. An organizational market consisting of firms that buy goods that are either converted into products or used during production.

_____ 22. The reasons for purchasing a product that are based on a logical evaluation of product attributes.

_____ 23. A group of products that a firm makes available for sale.

_____ 24. Intangible goods, such as time, expertise, or an activity, that can be purchased.

_____ 25. A group of closely related products that function in a similar manner or are sold to the same customer group who will use the products in similar ways.

_____ 26. A strategy of introducing new products to respond quickly to market changes.

_____ 27. The outside factors that influence marketing programs by posing opportunities or threats.

_____ 28. The process of dividing a market into categories of customer types.

_____ 29. The organizational market consisting of such nongovernmental buyers of goods and services as hospitals, churches, museums, and charitable organizations.

_____ 30. An industrial product purchased and consumed rapidly and regularly for daily operations.

_____ 31. A product that is dissimilar to those of competitors but that can fulfill the same need.

_____ 32. A pattern of regular consumer purchasing based on satisfaction with a product.

_____ 33. The physical container in which a product is sold, advertised, or protected.

_____ 34. The competitive marketing of domestic products against foreign products.

_____ 35. An expensive, rarely purchased product.

_____ 36. A good, service, or idea that is marketed to fill consumer needs and wants.

Let's List

1. List five factors in a company's external environment.
   a. _____
   b. _____
   c. _____
   d. _____
   e. _____

2. Marketing strives to provide four kinds of utility. Name them.
   a. _____
   b. _____
   c. _____
   d. _____

3. In identifying market segments, what are three of the most important influences of market behavior for people?
   a. _____
   b. _____
   c. _____

4. Organizational markets fall into what three categories?

    d. _____

    e. _____

    f. _____

5. List three categories of consumer goods.

    a. _____

    b. _____

    c. _____

6. List two classifications of industrial products.

    a. _____

    b. _____

7. List three types of brand names.

    a. _____

    b. _____

    c. _____

Let's Label

1. Label the stages of the product life cycle and give characteristics of each.

Stage:	1. _____	2. _____	3. _____	4. _____

Characteristics of Stage 1: _____
_____

Characteristics of Stage 2: _____
_____

Characteristics of Stage 3: _____
_____

Characteristics of Stage 4: _____
_____

Learning Objectives—Short Answer or Essay Questions

Learning Objective #1: Explain the concept of marketing and identify the five forces that constitute the external marketing environment.

Learning Objective #2: Explain the purpose of a marketing plan and identify the four components of the marketing mix.

Learning Objective #3: Explain market segmentation and how it is used in target marketing.

Learning Objective #4: Describe the key factors that influence the consumer buying process.

Learning Objective #5: Discuss the three categories of organizational markets.

Learning Objective #6: Explain the definition of a product as a value package and classify goods and services.

Learning Objective #7: Describe the key considerations in the new product development process.

Learning Objective #8: Explain the importance of branding and packaging.

Learning Objective #9: Discuss the challenges that arise in adopting an international marketing mix.

Learning Objective #10: Identify the ways that small businesses can benefit from an understanding of the marketing mix.

Critical Thinking Question

Describe how products are viewed by the consumer in terms of their value and benefits.

Brain Teaser

Why are product placements an effective branding strategy?

ANSWERS

True-False—Answers

1. True
2. False: Firms that sell products to other manufacturers engage in *industrial* marketing.
3. False: The *sociocultural* environment of marketing includes the context within which people's values, beliefs, and ideas affect marketing decisions.
4. False: The *economic* environment of marketing consists of the conditions, such as inflation, recession, and interest rates, that influence consumer and organizational spending patterns.
5. True
6. False: *International* competition is competitive marketing of domestic products against foreign products.
7. True
8. True
9. True
10. False: The components of the marketing mix are price, promotion, place, and *product*.
11. False: Marketing begins with a product—a good, service, or idea designed to fill a consumer need.
12. True
13. True
14. True
15. False: Market segmentation is designed to *divide the total market into smaller, relatively* homogenous groups.
16. False: *Psychographic* segmentation is the classification of customers on the basis of their psychological makeup.
17. True
18. True
19. True
20. True
21. False: *Organizational (or commercial)* markets are markets in which customers buy goods or services for resale or for use in conducting their own operations.
22. True

Multiple Choice—Answers

1. d	4. c	7. d	10. c	13. b	16. a
2. a	5. b	8. c	11. a	14. a	17. d
3. b	6. a	9. a	12. c	15. b	

Matching the Terms and Concepts with their Definitions—Answers

1. w	6. e	11. l	16. n	21. ff	26. dd	31. g	36. k
2. bb	7. p	12. c	17. ee	22. v	27. f	32. u	
3. r	8. gg	13. t	18. x	23. cc	28. o	33. jj	
4. a	9. y	14. q	19. b	24. d	29. hh	34. i	
5. h	10. ii	15. j	20. m	25. s	30. aa	35. z	

Let's List—Answers

1. List five factors in a company's external environment.
   a. Political-legal
   b. Sociocultural
   c. Technological
   d. Economic
   e. Competitive

2. Marketing strives to provide four kinds of utility. Name them.
   a. Time
   b. Place
   c. Ownership
   d. Form

3. In identifying market segments, what are three of the most important influences of market behavior for people?
   a. Geographic variables
   b. Demographic variables
   c. Psychographic variables

4. Organizational markets fall into what three categories?
   a. Industrial
   b. Reseller
   c. Government/institutional

5. List three categories of consumer goods.
   a. Convenience
   b. Shopping
   c. Specialty

6. List two classifications of industrial products.
   a. Expense items
   b. Capital items

7. List three types of brand names.
   a. National brands
   b. Licensed brands
   c. Private brands

Let's Label—Answers

1. Label the stages of the product life cycle and give characteristics of each.

Stage:	1. Introductory	2. Growth	3. Maturity	4. Decline

Characteristics of the **Introductory Stage**: The product reaches the marketplace. Marketers focus on making potential consumers aware of the product and its benefits. Extensive promotional and development costs erase all profits.

Characteristics of the **Growth Stage**: If the new product attracts enough consumers, sales start to climb sharply. The product starts to show a profit, and other firms move rapidly to introduce their own versions.

Characteristics of the **Maturity Stage**: Sales growth starts to slow. Although the product earns its highest profit level early in this stage, increased competition eventually forces price cutting and lower profits. Toward the end of the stage, sales start to fall.

Characteristics of the **Decline Stage**: Sales and profits continue to fall as new products in the introduction stage take away sales. Firms end or reduce promotional support (ads and salespeople), but may let the product linger to provide some profits.

Learning Objectives—Short Answer or Essay Questions—Answers

Learning Objective #1: Explain the concept of marketing and identify the five forces that constitute the external marketing environment.
According to the American Marketing Association, *marketing* is the process of planning and executing the conception, pricing, promotion, and distribution of ideas, goods, and services to create exchanges that satisfy individual and organizational objectives. The *external environment* consists of the outside forces that influence marketing strategy and decision making. The *political-legal environment* includes laws and regulations, both domestic and foreign, that may define or constrain business activities. The *sociocultural environment* is the context within which people's values, beliefs, and ideas affect marketing decisions. The *technological environment* includes the technological

developments that affect existing and new products. The *economic environment* consists of the conditions, such as inflation, recession, and interest rates, that influence both consumer and organizational spending patters. Finally, the *competitive environment* is the environment in which marketers must persuade buyers to purchase their products rather than those of their competitors.

Learning Objective #2: Explain the purpose of a marketing plan and identify the four components of the marketing mix.

A *marketing plan* is a detailed strategy for focusing marketing efforts on consumer needs and wants. A marketing strategy begins when a company identifies a consumer need and develops a product to meet it. The marketing mix includes product, pricing, place, and promotion. *Product* is a good, a service, or an idea designed to fill a consumer need or want. *Pricing* is selecting the best price at which to sell. *Place (or distribution)* includes placing a product in the proper outlet. *Promotion* refers to techniques for communicating information about products.

Learning Objective #3: Explain market segmentation and how it is used in target marketing.

Market segmentation is the process of dividing markets into categories of customers. Businesses have learned that marketing is more successful when it is aimed toward specific *target markets*: groups of consumers with similar wants and needs. Markets may be segmented by *geographic, demographic,* or *psychographic variables.*

Learning Objective #4: Describe the key factors that influence the consumer buying process.

One consumer behavior model considers five influences that lead to consumption: (1) *Problem/need recognition*: The buying process begins when the consumer recognizes a problem or need. (2) *Information seeking*: Having recognized a need, consumers seek information. (3) *Evaluation of alternatives*: Consumers compare products to decide which product best meets their needs. (4) *Purchase decision*: "Buy" decisions are based on rational motives, emotional motives, or both. *Rational motives* involve the logical evaluation of product attributes, such as cost, quality, and usefulness. *Emotional motives* involve nonobjective factors and include sociability, imitation of others, and aesthetics. (5) *Postpurchase evaluations*: Marketers want consumers to be happy after the consumption of products so that they are more likely to buy them again.

Learning Objective #5: Discuss the three categories of organizational markets.

The *industrial market* includes firms that buy goods falling into one of two categories: goods to be converted into other products and goods that are used up during production. Farmers and manufacturers are members of the industrial market. Members of the *reseller market* (mostly wholesalers) are intermediaries who buy and resell finished goods. Besides governments and agencies at all levels, the *government and institutional market* includes such nongovernment organizations as hospitals, museums, and charities. There are two main differences between consumer and organizational buying behavior: First, organizational buyers are typically professionals, specialists, or experts. Second, they often develop enduring buyer–seller relationships.

Learning Objective #6: Explain the definition of a product as a value package and classify goods and services.

Product *features*—the tangible and intangible qualities that a company builds into its products—offer benefits to buyers whose purchases are the main source of most company's profits. In developing products, firms must decide whether to produce *consumer goods* for direct sale to individual consumers or *industrial goods* for sale to other firms. Marketers must recognize that buyers will pay less for common, rapidly consumed, *convenience goods* than for less frequently purchased *shopping* and *specialty goods*. In industrial markets, *expense items* are generally less expensive and more rapidly consumed than such *capital items* as buildings and equipment.

Learning Objective #7: Describe the key considerations in the new product development process.

To expand or diversify product lines, new products must be developed and introduced. Many firms have research and development departments for continuously exploring new product possibilities because high mortality rates for new ideas result in only a few new products reaching the market. *Speed to market*— how fast a firm responds to market changes with new products —determines a product's profitability and success. A continuous product development process is necessary because every product has a *product life cycle*—a series of stages through which it passes during its commercial life.

Learning Objective #7: Explain the importance of branding and packaging.

Branding is a process of using symbols to communicate the qualities of a particular product made by a particular producer. Brands are designed to signal uniform quality. Customers who try and like a product can return to it by remembering its name. *Packaging* is a physical container in which a product is sold, advertised, or protected.

Learning Objective #9: Discuss the challenges that arise in adopting an international marketing mix.

If they go global, marketers must reconsider each element of the marketing mix—product, pricing, place, and promotion—because foreign customers differ from domestic buyers in language, customs, business practices, and consumer behavior. While some products can be sold abroad with virtually no changes, others require major redesign. When pricing for international markets, marketers must consider differences in the costs of transporting and selling products abroad. In some industries, delays in starting new international distribution networks can be costly, so companies with existing distribution systems enjoy an advantage. Often, U.S. promotional tactics do not succeed in other countries, so different promotional methods must be developed. Product promotions, therefore, must be carefully matched to local customs and cultural values.

Learning Objective #10: Identify the ways that small businesses can benefit from an understanding of the marketing mix.

Each element in the marketing mix—product, price, place, and promotion—can determine success or failure for any small business. Many *products* are failures because consumers don't need or want what they have to offer. A more realistic market potential can be gained by getting a clearer picture of what target segments want in a new product.

Small-business *pricing* errors usually result from a failure to estimate operating expenses accurately. By carefully assessing costs, small businesses can set prices that earn satisfactory profits. Perhaps the most crucial aspect of *place*, or distribution, for small businesses is location because it determines the ability to attract customers. Although *promotion* can be expensive and is essential for small businesses, especially at startup, costs can be reduced by using less expensive promotional methods. Local newspaper articles and television cover business events, thus providing free public exposure.

Critical Thinking Question—Answer

Describe how products are viewed by the consumer in terms of their value and benefits.

The value of a product compares its benefits with its costs. Benefits include not only the functions of the product, but also the emotional satisfaction associated with owning, experiencing, or possessing it.

Brain Teaser—Answer

Why are product placements an effective branding strategy?

Product placements are effective because the message is delivered in an attractive setting that holds the consumer's interest. When used in successful films and TV shows, the brand's association with famous performers is an implied celebrity endorsement.

Chapter 12
Pricing, Distributing, and Promoting Products

Learning Objectives
After reading this chapter, you should be able to:

1. Identify the various pricing objectives that govern pricing decisions and describe the price-setting tools used in making these decisions.
2. Discuss pricing strategies that can be used for different competitive situations and identify the pricing tactics that can be used for setting prices.
3. Explain the meaning of *distribution mix* and identify the different channels of distribution.
4. Describe the role of wholesalers and explain the different types of retailing.
5. Describe the role of e-intermediaries and explain how they add value for advertisers and consumers on the Internet.
6. Define *physical distribution* and describe the major activities in the physical distribution process.
7. Identify the important objectives of promotion, discuss the considerations in selecting a promotional mix, and discuss advertising promotions.
8. Outline the tasks involved in personal selling, describe the various types of sales promotions, and distinguish between publicity and public relations.

True-False
Indicate whether the statement is generally true or false by placing a "T" or an "F" in the space provided. If it is a false statement, correct it so that it becomes a true statement.

_____ 1. Markup is the amount added to an item's cost to sell it at a profit.

_____ 2. A variable cost is any cost that does not change with the production level.

_____ 3. Breakeven analysis attempts to determine the quantity of a product that must be sold before a profit is made.

_____ 4. Penetration pricing is setting an initial high price to cover new product costs and generate a profit.

_____ 5. Price lining is setting a limited number of prices for certain categories of products.

_____ 6. Psychological pricing appeals to buyers' perceptions of relative prices.

_____ 7. Discounting is reducing prices to stimulate sales.

_____ 8. Two general values to be gained from any promotional activity are communicating information and creating more satisfied customers.

_____ 9. The ultimate goal of any promotion is to reduce costs of production.

_____ 10. Positioning a product means establishing an identifiable image in consumers' minds.

_____ 11. Some of the more important promotional tools are personal selling, advertising, sales promotions, and public relations.

_____ 12. Personal selling includes order processing, creative selling, and missionary selling.

_____ 13. Missionary selling is the promotion of a firm and its products rather than trying to close sales.

_____ 14. Coupons, point-of-purchase displays, premiums, and trade shows are all types of advertising.

_____ 15. Intermediaries are generally classified as being wholesalers or retailers.

_____ 16. Retailers sell products to other businesses that then resell them to final consumers, while wholesalers sell products directly to consumers.

_____ 17. A distribution channel is the path that a product follows from producer to end-user.

_____ 18. The distribution of consumer products can travel through direct channels, through a retailer, wholesaler, or agent/broker.

_____ 19. A sales agent is an independent intermediary who generally deals in the related product lines of a few producers and forms long-term relationships to represent those producers and meet the needs of steady customers.

_____ 20. Generally, nondirect distribution channels mean a higher price for end users; the more members in the channel—the more intermediaries—the higher the final price.

Multiple Choice
Circle the best answer for each of the following questions.

1. Breakeven analysis
   a. attempts to find that volume of production for which variable costs equal fixed costs.
   b. determines the quantity of a product that must be sold before a profit can be earned.
   c. determines the amount of markup required in order to earn a profit.
   d. All of the above.

2. Which of the following statements is *true*?
   a. Price skimming is charging a high price for a new product during the introductory stage and lowering the price later.
   b. Penetration pricing is introducing a new product at a low price in hopes of building sales volume quickly.
   c. Price lining means offering all items in certain categories at a limited number of prices.
   d. All of the above.

3. Odd-even pricing is
   a. a price reduction offered as an incentive to purchase.
   b. setting a limited number of prices for certain categories of products.
   c. a psychological pricing tactic based on the premise that customers prefer prices not stated in even dollar amounts.
   d. setting an initial low price to establish a new product in the market.

4. Setting an initial high price to cover new product costs and generate a profit is known as
   a. penetration pricing.   b. discounting.
   c. price lining.   d. price skimming.

5. Which of the following is NOT part of the promotional mix?
   a. Personal selling   b. Pricing
   c. Advertising   d. Public relations

6. Promotion seeks to accomplish which of the following things with customers?
   a. Make them aware and knowledgeable of products
   b. Persuade them to like products
   c. Persuade them to purchase products
   d. All of the above.

7. Marketers may use promotion to
    a. communicate information.   b. position products.
    c. add value and to control sales volume. d. All of the above.

8. The personal selling task in which salespeople receive orders and see to their handling and delivery is called
    a. closing.   b. creative selling.
    c. order processing.   d. missionary selling.

9. Personal selling
    a. involves direct, person-to-person communication, either face-to-face or by phone.
    b. has the disadvantage of being relatively expensive.
    c. has the advantage of allowing for immediate interaction between buyers and sellers, and enables sellers to adjust their message to the specific needs and interests of their individual customers.
    d. All of the above.

10. A sales promotion technique in which offers of free or reduced-price items are used to stimulate purchases is called a
    a. premium.
    b. trade show.
    c. point-of-purchase display.
    d. coupon.

11. Which of the following is *true*?
    a. The global perspective to international advertising directs its marketing to local or regional markets.
    b. Publicity is a promotional tool in which information about a company or product is transmitted by general mass media.
    c. Rarely do large companies undertake public relations.
    d. All of the above.

12. Whether a firm relies on independent intermediaries or uses its own distribution networks and sales forces hinges on
    a. the company's target markets.
    b. the nature of its product.
    c. the cost of maintaining distribution and sales networks.
    d. All of the above.

13. Which of the following describes a type of distribution channel?
    a. Producer to consumer
    b. Producer to retailer to consumer
    c. Producer to wholesaler to retailer to consumer
    d. All of the above.

14. Which of the following statements is *true*?
   a. A factory outlet is a bargain retailer offering large discounts on brand-name merchandise to customers who have paid annual membership fees.
   b. Retailers can be described according to two classifications: product line retailers and bargain retailers.
   c. A specialty store is a large product line retailer carrying a wide variety of unrelated products.
   d. All of the above.

15. Which of the following is a type of nonstore retailer?
   a. Electronic storefronts   b. Discount stores
   c. Specialty stores   d. Supermarkets

Match the Terms and Concepts with Their Definitions

a. pricing
b. pricing objectives
c. market share
d. markup
e. variable cost
f. fixed cost
g. breakeven analysis
h. breakeven point
i. price skimming
j. penetration pricing
k. psychological pricing
l. odd-even pricing
m. discount

n. promotion

o. positioning
p. promotional mix
q. advertising
r. advertising media

s. premium
t. personal selling
u. creative selling
v. missionary selling
w. sales promotion
x. coupon
y. point-of-sale display
z. premium
aa. trade show
bb. publicity
cc. public relations
dd. distribution mix
ee. intermediary

ff. wholesaler

gg. retailer
hh. distribution channel
ii. direct channel
jj. cost-oriented pricing

kk. wholesalers
ll. media mix
mm. private warehouse
nn. department store
oo. supermarket
pp. specialty store
qq. bargain retailer
rr. discount house
ss. catalog showroom
tt. factory outlet
uu. wholesale club
vv. convenience store
ww. direct-response retailing
xx. mail order (catalog marketing)
yy. telemarketing
zz. direct selling

_____ 1. The assessment of the quantity of a product that must be sold before the seller makes profit.

_____ 2. Setting an initial low price to establish a new product in the market.

_____ 3. The price reduction offered as an incentive to purchase.

_____ 4. An amount added to an item's cost to sell it at a profit.

_____ 5. The cost unaffected by the quantity of a product produced or sold.

_____ 6. The process of determining what a company will receive in exchange for its products.

_____ 7. The quantity of a product that must be sold before the seller covers variable and fixed costs and makes a profit.

_____ 8. The psychological pricing tactic based on the premise that customers prefer prices not stated in even dollar amounts.

_____ 9. The pricing tactic that takes advantage of the fact that consumers do not always respond rationally to stated prices.

_____ 10. The cost that changes with the quantity of a product produced or sold.

_____ 11. As a percentage, the total of market sales for a specific company or product.

_____ 12. Setting an initial high price to cover new product costs and generate a profit.

_____ 13. The goals that producers hope to attain in pricing products for sale.

_____ 14. The sales-promotion technique in which offers of free or reduced-price items are used to stimulate purchases.

_____ 15. Company-influenced publicity directed at building goodwill between an organization and potential customers.

_____ 16. The personal selling tasks in which salespeople promote their firms and products rather than try to close sales.

_____ 17. The process of establishing an identifiable product image in the minds of consumers.

_____ 18. A promotional tool in which information about a company or product is transmitted by general mass media.

_____ 19. The short-term promotional activity designed to stimulate consumer buying or cooperation from distributors and sales agents.

_____ 20. An aspect of the marketing mix concerned with the most effective techniques for selling a product.

_____ 21. A sales-promotion technique in which product displays are located in certain areas to stimulate purchase.

_____ 22. A combination of tools used to promote a product.

_____ 23. The personal selling task in which salespeople try to persuade buyers to purchase products by providing information about their benefits.

_____ 24. The sales-promotion technique in which various members of an industry gather to display, demonstrate, and sell products.

_____ 25. A promotional tool consisting of paid, nonpersonal communication used by an identified sponsor to inform an audience about a product.

_____ 26. The sales-promotion technique in which offers of free or reduced-price items are used to stimulate purchases.

_____ 27. The sales-promotion technique in which a certificate is issued entitling the buyer to a reduced price.

_____ 28. Communication devices for carrying a seller's message to potential customers.

_____ 29. A promotional tool in which a salesperson communicates one-on-one with potential customers.

_____ 30. A large product line retailer characterized by organization into specialized departments.

_____ 31. An intermediary who sells products directly to consumers.

_____ 32. Nonstore retailing by direct interaction with customers to inform them of products and to receive sales orders.

_____ 33. A bargain retailer that generates large sales volume by offering goods at substantial price reductions.

_____ 34. A channel in which a product travels from producer to consumer without intermediaries.

_____ 35. Provide a variety of services to buyers of products for resale or business use.

_____ 36. A bargain retailer offering large discounts on brand-name merchandise to customers who have paid annual membership fees.

_____ 37. A small retail store carrying one product line or category of related products.

_____ 38. An individual or firm that helps to distribute a product.

_____ 39. A bargain retailer in which customers place orders for catalog items to be picked up at on-premises warehouses.

_____ 40. Pricing that considers the firm's desire to make a profit and its need to cover production costs.

_____ 41. A form of nonstore retailing typified by door-to-door sales.

_____ 42. An independent wholesaler who takes legal possession of goods produced by a variety of manufacturers and then resells them to other businesses.

_____ 43. A warehouse owned by and providing storage for a single company.

_____ 44. A retailer carrying a wide range of products at bargain prices.

_____ 45. A large product line retailer offering a variety of food and food-related items in specialized departments.

_____ 46. A combination of distribution channels by which a firm gets its products to end users.

_____ 47. A combination of advertising media chosen to carry a message about a product.

_____ 48. Interdependent companies through which a product passes from producer to end user.

_____ 49. Nonstore retailing in which the telephone is used to sell directly to consumers.

_____ 50. An intermediary who sells products to other businesses for resale to final consumers.

_____ 51. A bargain retailer owned by the manufacturer whose products it sells.

_____ 52. A retail store offering easy accessibility, extended hours, and fast service.

Learning Objectives—Short Answer or Essay Questions

Learning Objective #1: Identify the various pricing objectives that govern pricing decisions and describe the price-setting tools used in making these decisions.

Learning Objective #2: Discuss pricing strategies that can be used for different competitive situations and identify the pricing tactics that can be used for setting prices.

Learning Objective #3: Explain the meaning of *distribution mix* and identify the different channels of distribution.

Learning Objective #4: Describe the role of wholesalers and explain the different types of retailing.

Learning Objective #5 Describe the role of e-intermediaries and explain how they add value for advertisers and consumers on the Internet.

Learning Objective #6: Define *physical distribution* and describe the major activities in the physical distribution process.

Learning Objective #7: Identify the important objectives for promotion, discuss the considerations in selecting a promotional mix, and discuss advertising promotions.

Learning Objective #8: Outline the tasks involved in personal selling, describe the various types of sales promotions, and distinguish between publicity and public relations.

Critical Thinking Question

Describe the common functions that can be provided by wholesalers.

Brain Teaser

Explain some of the disadvantages associated with the use of publicity in promoting products.

ANSWERS

True-False—Answers

1. True
2. False: A *fixed* cost is any cost that does not change with the production level.
3. True
4. False: *Price skimming* is setting an initial high price to cover new product costs and generate a profit.
5. True
6. True
7. True
8. True
9. False: The ultimate goal of any promotion is to *increase sales*.
10. True
11. True
12. True
13. True
14. False: Coupons, point-of-purchase displays, premiums, and trade shows are all types of *sales promotions*.
15. True
16. False: *Wholesalers* sell products to other businesses that then resell them to final customers, while *retailers* sell products directly to consumers.
17. True
18. True
19. True
20. True

Multiple Choice—Answers

1. b	4. d	7. d	10. a	13. d
2. d	5. b	8. c	11. b	14. b
3. c	6. d	9. d	12. d	15. a

Match the Terms and Concepts with Their Definitions—Answers

1. g	10. e	19. w	28. r	37. pp	46. dd
2. j	11. c	20. n	29. t	38. ee	47. ll
3. m	12. i	21. y	30. nn	39. ss	48. hh
4. d	13. b	22. p	31. gg	40. jj	49. yy
5. f	14. z	23. u	32. ww	41. zz	50. ff
6. a	15. cc	24. aa	33. rr	42. mm	51. tt
7. h	16. v	25. q	34. ii	43. xx	52. vv
8. l	17. o	26. s	35. kk	44. qq	
9. k	18. bb	27. x	36. uu	45. oo	

Learning Objectives—Short Answer or Essay Questions—Answers

Learning Objective #1: Identify the various pricing objectives that govern pricing decisions and describe the price-setting tools used in making these decisions.
Two major pricing objectives are as follows: (1) *Pricing to maximize profits*: With prices set too low, the seller misses the chance to make additional profits on each of the many units sold. With prices set too high, a larger profit will be made on each unit, but fewer units will be sold. (2) *Market share objectives*: Pricing is used for establishing market share. The seller is willing to accept minimal profits, even losses, to get buyers to try products. Two basic tools are as follows: (1) *Cost-oriented pricing* begins by determining total costs for making products available to shoppers, then a figure for profit is added in to arrive at selling price. (2) *Breakeven analysis* assesses total costs versus revenues for various sales volumes. It shows, at each possible sales volume, the amount of loss or profit for any chosen sales price. It also shows the *breakeven point*: the number of sales units for total revenue to equal total costs.

Learning Objective #2: Discuss pricing strategies that can be used for different competitive situations and identify the pricing tactics that can be used for setting prices.
Pricing for existing products can be set above, at, or below market prices for similar products. High pricing is often interpreted as meaning higher quality and prestige, while low pricing may attract greater sales volume. Strategies for new products include *price skimming*—setting an initially high price to cover costs and generate a profit—and *penetration pricing*—setting a low price to establish a new product in the market. Strategies for e-businesses include dynamic versus fixed pricing. *Dynamic pricing* establishes individual prices by real-time interaction the seller with each customer on the Internet. *Fixed pricing* is the traditional one-price-for-all arrangement.

Three tactics are often used for setting prices: (1) With *price lining*, any product category (such as shoes) will be set at three or four price levels and all shoes will be priced at one of those levels. (2) *Psychological pricing* acknowledges that customers are not completely rational when making buying decisions, as with odd-even pricing where customers regard prices such as $10 as being significantly higher than $9.95. (3) *Discount pricing* uses price reductions to stimulate sales.

Learning Objective #3: Explain the meaning of *distribution mix* and identify the different channels of distribution.
The combination of distribution channels for getting products to end users—consumers and industrial buyers—is the *distribution mix*. *Intermediaries* help to distribute a producer's goods by moving them from sellers to customers: *Wholesalers* sell products to other businesses, which resell them to final users. *Retailers*, *sales agents*, and *brokers* sell products directly to end users. In the simplest of four distribution channels, the producer sells directly to users. Channel 2 includes a retailer, Channel 3 involves both a retailer and a wholesaler, and Channel 4 includes an agent or broker.

Learning Objective #4: Describe the role of wholesalers and explain the different types of retailing.

Wholesalers provide a variety of services—delivery, credit arrangements, and product information—to buyers of products for resale or business use. In buying and reselling an assortment of products, wholesalers provide storage, marketing advice, and assist customers by marking prices and setting up displays. *Retail stores* range from broad product-line department stores and supermarkets, to small specialty stores for specific market segments seeking narrow product lines. With retail stores, there is always an intermediary that moves products from producers to users. Various kinds of nonstore retailing include *direct-response retailing*, *mail order* (or *catalog marketing*), *telemarketing*, and *direct selling*. Many nonstore retailers do not use intermediaries but, instead, use direct-to-consumer contact by the producer.

Learning Objective #5: Describe the role of e-intermediaries and explain how they add value for advertisers and consumers on the Internet.

E-intermediaries are Internet-based channel members who perform one or both of two functions: (1) they collect information about sellers and present it to consumers, and (2) they help deliver Internet products to buyers. There are three types of e-intermediaries: (1) *Syndicated selling* occurs when a Web site offers other Web sites a commission for referring customers. (2) *Shopping agents* (*e-agents*) help Internet consumers by gathering and sorting information (such as comparison prices and product features) for making purchases. They add value for sellers by listing sellers' Web addresses for consumers. (3) *Electronic retailers* use the Internet to interact with customers to inform, sell to, and distribute products to them. *E-catalogs* are electronic displays that give instant world-wide access to pages of product information. *Electronic storefronts* and *cybermalls* provide collections of virtual storefronts at which Internet shoppers collect information about products, place orders, and pay for purchases.

Learning Objective #6: Define *physical distribution* and describe the major activities in the physical distribution process.

Physical distribution is all activities needed to move products from producers to consumers, making them available when and where customers want, at reasonable cost. Physical distribution activities include providing customer services, warehousing, and transportation of products. Warehouses provide storage for products, whereas transportation operations physically move products from suppliers to customers. Trucks, railroads, planes, water carriers (boats and barges), and pipelines are the major transportation modes used in the distribution process.

Learning Objective #7: Identify the important objectives of promotion, discuss the considerations in selecting a promotional mix, and discuss advertising promotions.

Although the ultimate goal of promotion is to increase sales, other goals include communicating information, positioning a product, adding value, and controlling sales volume. In deciding on the appropriate *promotional mix*—the best combination of promotional tools (e.g., advertising, personal selling, public relations)—marketers must consider the good or service being offered, characteristics of the target audience, the buyer's decision process, and the promotional mix budget. *Advertising* is paid, nonpersonal communication, by which an identified sponsor informs an audience about a product. Marketers use several different advertising media—specific communication devices for carrying a seller's message to potential customers—each having its advantages and drawbacks. The combination of media through which a company advertises is called its *media mix*.

Learning Objective #8: Outline the tasks involved in personal selling, describe the various types of sales promotions, and distinguish between publicity and public relations.

Personal selling tasks include *order processing*, *creative selling*, and *missionary selling*. Sales promotions include *point-of-sale (POS)* displays to attract consumer attention, help them find products in stores, and provide product information. Other sales promotions give purchasing incentives such as *samples* (customers can try products without having to buy them), *coupons* (a certificate for price reduction), and *premiums* (free or reduced-price rewards for buying products). At *trade shows*, B2B sellers rent booths to display products to industrial customers. *Contests* intend to stimulate sales, with prizes to high-producing intermediaries and consumers who use the seller's products.

Publicity is information about a company, a product, or an event transmitted by the general mass media to attract public attention. Control of the message's content is determined by outside writers and reporters. In contrast to publicity, *public relations* is company-influenced information that seeks to either build good relations with the public or to deal with unfavorable events.

Critical Thinking Question—Answer

Describe the common functions that can be provided by wholesalers.

Wholesalers can provide storage, delivery, and additional value-adding services, including credit, marketing advice, and merchandising services, such as marking prices and setting up displays.

Brain Teaser—Answer

Explain some of the disadvantages associated with the use of publicity in promoting products.

While publicity is free, marketers have no control over the content media reporters and writers disseminate, and because it is presented in a news format, consumers often regard it as objective and credible.

Chapter 13
Information Technology for Business

Learning Objectives
After reading this chapter, you should be able to:

1. Discuss the impacts information technology has had on the business world.
2. Identify the IT resources businesses have at their disposal and how these resources are used.
3. Describe the role of information systems, the different types of information systems, and how businesses use such systems.
4. Identify the threats and risks information technology poses on businesses.
5. Describe the ways in which businesses protect themselves from the threats and risks information technology poses.

True-False
Indicate whether the statement is generally true or false by placing a "T" or an "F" in the space provided. If it is a false statement, correct it so that it becomes a true statement.

_____ 1. The management of a firm's information system is a core activity because all of a firm's business activities are linked to it.

_____ 2. Data is a meaningful, useful interpretation of information.

_____ 3. An Internet service provider (ISP) is a commercial firm that maintains a permanent connection to the Internet and sells temporary connections to subscribers.

_____ 4. The World Wide Web is a system with universally accepted standards for storing, formatting, retrieving, and displaying information.

_____ 5. The Internet is the world's largest computer network.

_____ 6. The rapid growth of information technologies has had little impact on the structure of business organizations.

_____ 7. The rapid growth of information technologies has resulted in leaner organizations characterized by geographic separation of the workplace and company headquarters.

169

_____ 8. The rapid growth of information technologies has resulted in less collaboration among internal units of a company and outside firms.

_____ 9. Each business function—marketing, human resources, accounting, production, and finance—has the same information requirements.

_____ 10. Enterprise resource planning (ERP) is a large information system for integrating all of the activities of a company's business units.

_____ 11. VSAT satellite communications is a network of geographically dispersed transceivers that sends and receives video signals only.

_____ 12. Computer-aided design (CAD) is a computer-based technology that assists in designing products by simulating a real product and displaying it in three-dimensional graphics.

_____ 13. Information systems for knowledge workers and office applications include personal productivity tools such as word processing, document imaging, desktop publishing, computer-aided design, and simulation modeling.

_____ 14. E-commerce uses the Internet and other electronic means for retailing and business-to-business transactions.

_____ 15. Information technology creates entirely new businesses but does little for existing businesses.

_____ 16. Software includes the physical devices and components, including the computer, in the information system.

Multiple Choice

Circle the best answer for each of the following questions.

1. Information systems
    a. enable managers to collect, process, and transmit information for use in decision making.
    b. provide the technology to convert data into desired information.
    c. are crucial in planning.
    d. All of the above.

2. Which of the following statements is *true*?
    a. Databases consist of fields, records, and files.
    b. Most business application programs fall into one of four categories—word processing, spreadsheets, database management, and graphics.
    c. An electronic spreadsheet is an applications program with a row-and-column format that allows users to store, manipulate, and compare numeric data.
    d. All of the above.

3. A software and hardware system that prevents outsiders from accessing a company's internal network is called
   a. a firewall.   b. a search engine.
   c. a browser.   d. a Web server.

4. Software supporting the graphics and linking capabilities necessary to navigate the World Wide Web is
   a. a search engine.   b. a firewall.
   c. a browser.   d. an extranet.

5. As a result of growth in information technologies, companies are
   a. leaning to organizations with more employees and more complicated organizational structures.
   b. offering customers less variety and slower delivery cycles.
   c. changing the very nature of the management process.
   d. more likely to hire more employees to work at one central location.

6. Top-level managers are most likely to use which of the following general types of information systems?
   a. Strategic information systems   b. Management information systems
   c. Knowledge information systems   d. Operational information systems

7. An application program for creating, storing, searching, and manipulating an organized collection of data is called
   a. a word-processing program.   b. a database management program.
   c. an electronic spreadsheet.   d. a computer graphics program.

8. The impacts of IT include all of the following EXCEPT
   a. providing remote access to instant information.
   b. enabling better service by coordinating remote deliveries.
   c. creating leaner, more efficient organizations.
   d. enabling decreased collaboration.

9. Which of the following statements is *true*?
   a. Management information systems (MISs) support an organization's managers by providing daily reports, schedules, plans, and budgets.
   b. An information system (IS) is a system that uses IT resources and enables managers to take data and turn that it into information.
   c. Decision-support systems (DSS) are interactive applications that assist the decision-making process of middle- and top-managers.
   d. All of the above.

10. Which of the following is software?
    a. An input device such as a keyboard
    b. A central processing unit
    c. Applications programs such as word processing, spreadsheets, or Web browsers
    d. Output device such as a video monitor or printer

Match the Terms and Concepts with Their Definitions

a. encryption system
b. VSAT satellite communications
c. groupware
d. router
e. post office protocol

f. knowledge workers
g. electronic conferencing
h. identity theft
i. computer-aided design (CAD)
j. decision support system (DSS)
k. data warehousing
l. hacker
m. computer network
n. client-server network
o. hypertext transfer protocol (HTTP)
p. data
q. information

r. information system (IS)
s. management information system (MIS)
t. Blackberry
u. extranet
v. networks

w. Microsoft Windows Vista

x. wireless WAN
y. hardware
z. data mining
aa. software
bb. data
cc. application software
dd. wireless LAN
ee. firewall

ff. worms
gg. software

hh. spyware
ii. knowledge information system
jj. spam
kk. IS managers
ll. simple message transfer protocol

mm. wide area network (WA
nn. local area network (LAN
oo. Wi-Fi
pp. anti-virus software
qq. intellectual property
rr. mass customization
ss. e-commerce
tt. Internet
uu. World Wide Web
vv. information technology

ww. Intranet

_____ 1. The unauthorized stealing of personal information (such as a social security number and address) to get loans, credit cards, or other monetary benefits by impersonating the victim.

_____ 2. Managers who operate the systems used for gathering, organizing, and distributing information.

_____ 3. The system software for PCs that tells the computer's hardware how to interact with the software.

_____ 4. A private network of internal Web sites and other sources of information available to a company's employees.

_____ 5. All of the computer and information technology devices that, by working together, drive the flow of digital information throughout a system.

_____ 6. A table of available routes or paths: a "traffic switch."

_____ 7. A network of geographically dispersed transmitter-receivers (transceivers) that send signals to and receive signals from a satellite, exchanging voice, video, and data transmissions.

_____ 8. A subsystem of computers providing access to the Internet and offering multimedia and linking capabilities.

_____ 9. An information system that supports knowledge workers by providing resources to create, store, use, and transmit new knowledge for useful applications.

_____ 10. An interactive computer-based system that locates and presents information needed to support decision making.

_____ 11. A smart phone that features wireless Internet access.

_____ 12. The various appliances and devices for creating, storing, exchanging, and using information in diverse modes, including visual images, voice, multimedia, and business data.

_____ 13. A virus that travels from computer to computer within networked computer systems.

_____ 14. Raw facts and figures.

_____ 15. Software that assigns an email message to a unique code number (digital fingerprint) for each computer so only that computer, not others, can open and read the message.

_____ 16. A network of computers and workstations, usually within a company, that are linked together by cable.

_____ 17. An information-technology system consisting of clients (users) that are electronically linked to share network resources provided by a server, such as a host computer.

_____ 18. The basic communications protocol used to send e-mail.

_____ 19. A global data communication network serving millions of computers with information on a wide array of topics and providing communication flows among certain private networks.

_____ 20. Employees who use information and knowledge as raw materials and who rely on information technology to design new products or business systems.

_____ 21. A cybercriminal who gains unauthorized access to a computer or network, either to steal information, money, or property, or to tamper with data.

_____ 22. Internet allowing outsiders access to a firm's internal information system.

_____ 23. A network of computers and workstations located far from one another and
           linked by telephone wires or by satellite.

_____ 24. The collection, storage, and retrieval of data in electronic files.

_____ 25. The communications protocol used for the worldwide web, in which related
           pieces of information on separate web pages are connected using hyperlinks.

_____ 26. A program unknowingly downloaded by users that monitors their computer
           activities, gathering email addresses, credit card numbers, and other
           information that it transmits to someone outside the host system.

_____ 27. A product of the mind—something produced by the intellect, with great
           expenditure of human effort—that has commercial value.

_____ 28. The application of electronic technologies for searching, sifting, and
           reorganizing pools of data to uncover useful information.

_____ 29. The use of the Internet and other electronic means for retailing and business-
           to-business transactions.

_____ 30. A physical components of a computer system.

_____ 31. A computer-based electronic technology that assists in designing products by
           simulating a real product and displaying it in three-dimensional graphics.

_____ 32. Junk email sent to a mailing list or a newsgroup.

_____ 33. One of the basic communications protocols used to receive e-mail.

_____ 34. A local area network with wireless access points for PC users.

_____ 35. A product that protects systems by searching incoming emails and data files
           for "signatures" of known viruses and virus-like characteristics.

_____ 36. The meaningful, useful interpretation of data.

_____ 37. The programs that tell the computer's hardware what resources to use, and
           how to use them.

_____ 38. The software that connects members of a group for shared e-mail distribution,
           electronic meetings, appointments, and group writing.

_____ 39. A computer-based system that allows people to communicate simultaneously
           from different locations via software or telephone.

_____ 40. Although companies produce in large volumes, each unit features the unique options the customer prefers.

_____ 41. A system for transforming raw data into information that can be used in decision making.

_____ 42. The software and hardware system that prevents outsiders from accessing a company's internal network.

_____ 43. The software (Microsoft Excel) that processes data according to a user's special needs.

_____ 44. A system used for transforming data into information for use in decision making.

_____ 45. Short for wireless fidelity; a wireless local area network.

_____ 46. Enable firms to maintain information linkages among employees and customers.

_____ 47. Programs that instruct a computer in what to do.

_____ 48. A network that uses airborne electronic signals instead of wires to link computers and electronic devices over long distances.

_____ 49. The raw facts and figures that, by themselves, may not have much meaning.

Let's List

1. List ways in which information networks help us free the workplace from physical constraints.
   a. _____
   b. _____
   c. _____
   d. _____
   e. _____

2. List other business communications technologies that the Internet has spawned.
   a. _____
   b. _____
   c. _____
   d. _____

3. List the ways networks can be classified.
   a. _____

b. _____

c. _____

d. _____

4. List five types of IT protection measures.

a. _____

b. _____

c. _____

d. _____

e. _____

Learning Objectives—Short Answer or Essay Question

Learning Objective #1 Discuss the impacts information technology has had on the business world.

Learning Objective #2 Identify the IT resources businesses have at their disposal and how these resources are used.

Learning Objective #3: Describe the role of information systems, the different types of information systems, and how businesses use such systems.

Learning Objective #4: Identify the threats and risks information technology poses on businesses.

Learning Objective #5: Describe the ways in which businesses protect themselves from the threats and risks information technology poses.

Critical Thinking Questions

1. Explain how data conferencing is used to save time and money.

2. How has information technology (IT) contributed to greater organizational efficiency?

Brain Teaser

Describe how managers use data mining.

ANSWERS

True-False—Answers

1. True
2. False: *Information* is a meaningful, useful interpretation of *data*.
3. True
4. True
5. True
6. False: The growth of information technologies has *changed* the structure of business organizations.
7. True
8. False: The rapid growth of information technologies has resulted in *more* collaboration among internal units of a company and outside firms.
9. False: Each business function—marketing, human resources, accounting, production, and finance—has *different* information requirements.
10. True
11. False: It is a network of geographically dispersed transceivers that sends and receives exchanging voice, video, and data transmissions.
12. True
13. True
14. True
15. False: It helps improve existing businesses as well as helps create new businesses.
16. False: *Hardware* includes the physical devices and components, including the computer, in the information system.

Multiple Choice—Answers

1. d	3. a	5. c	7. b	9. d
2. d	4. c	6. b	8. d	10. d

Match the Terms and Concepts with Their Definitions—Answers

1. h	11. t	21. l	31. i	41. r
2. kk	12. vv	22. u	32. jj	42. ee
3. w	13. ff	23. mm	33. e	43. cc
4. ww	14. p	24. k	34. dd	44. s
5. m	15. a	25. o	35. pp	45. oo
6. d	16. nn	26. hh	36. o	46. v
7. b	17. n	27. qq	37. gg	47. aa
8. uu	18. ll	28. z	38. c	48. x
9. ii	19. tt	29. ss	39. g	49. bb
10. j	20. f	30. y	40. rr	

Let's List—Answers

1. List ways in which information networks help us free the workplace from physical constraints.
   a. Leaner organization
   b. More flexible operations
   c. Increased collaboration
   d. Enabling global exchange
   e. Improved management processes

2. List the other business communications technologies that the Internet has spawned.
   a. Intranets
   b. Extranets
   c. Electronic conferencing
   d. VSAT satellite communications

3. List the ways networks can be classified.
   a. Wide area networks (WANs)
   b. Local area networks (LANs)
   c. Wireless wide area networks (WWANS)
   d. Wireless local area network (Wireless LAN or WLAN), known as Wi-Fi

4. List five types of IT protection measures.
   a. Firewalls
   b. Preventing identity theft
   c. Preventing viruses through anti-virus software
   d. Protecting electronic communication through encryption software
   e. Avoiding spam and spyware

Learning Objectives—Short Answer or Essay Questions—Answers

Learning Objective #1: Discuss the impacts information technology has had on the business world.
The growth of IT has changed the very structure of business organizations. Its adoption provides new modes of communication, including portable offices, resulting in the geographic separation of the workplace from headquarters for many employees. By providing instantaneous access to company information, IT has altered the workforces in many companies, enabling them to streamline with fewer employees and simpler structures. It also contributes to greater flexibility in serving customers and enables closer coordination with suppliers. IT's global reach facilitates project collaboration with remote business partners and the formation of new market relationships around the globe. Just as electronic collaboration has changed the way employees interact with each other, IT networks have created new manufacturing flexibility for mass customization, and Internet access has brought new opportunities for small businesses.

Learning Objective #2: Identify the IT resources businesses have at their disposal and how these resources are used.

The Internet and the Web serve computers with information and provide communication flows among networks around the world. For many businesses, the Internet is replacing the telephone, fax machine, and standard mail as the primary communications tool. To support internal communications, many companies maintain internal websites, *intranets,* accessible only to employees. Some firms give limited network access to outsiders via extranets for coordination with suppliers and customers. *VSAT satellite networks* provide private long-distance communications for voice, video, and data transmissions. Computer networks (wide area networks, local area networks) enable the sharing of information, hardware, software, and other resources over wired or wireless connections. Hardware refers to the computer's physical components. Software includes programs to meet specific user needs, such as groupware with voice and video connections for remote collaboration.

Learning Objective #3: Describe the role of information systems, the different types of information systems, and how businesses use such systems.

An *information system* enables users to collect, process, and transmit information for use in decision making. *Knowledge information systems* support knowledge workers by providing resources to create, store, use, and transmit new knowledge for useful applications. *Management information systems* support managers by providing reports, schedules, plans, and budgets that can then be used for making decisions at all levels ranging from detailed daily activities to long-range business strategy. The many uses of information systems include experimenting to test the effectiveness of potential decisions, data mining to identify shopping trends and to plan for new products, and planning delivery schedules from suppliers and to customers.

Learning Objective #4: Identify the threats and risks information technology poses on businesses.

IT has attracted abusers that do mischief, with severity ranging from mere nuisance to outright destruction, costing companies millions. Hackers break into computers, stealing personal information and company secrets, tampering with data, and launching attacks on other computers. Once inside a computer network, hackers are able to commit *identity theft*, the unauthorized stealing of personal information to get loans, credit cards, or other monetary benefits by impersonating the victim. Even the ease of information sharing on the Internet poses a threat: it has proven costly for companies who are having a difficult time protecting their intellectual property, such as software products, movies, and music. Another IT risk facing businesses is system shutdown and destruction of software, hardware, or data files by *viruses*, *worms*, and *Trojan horses*. *Spam* damage is also costly in terms of lost time and productivity.

Learning Objective #5: Describe the ways in which businesses protect themselves from the threats and risks information technology poses.

Most systems guard against unauthorized access by requiring users to have protected *passwords*. In addition, many firms rely on safeguards such as *firewalls* so that only messages that meet the conditions of the company's security policy are permitted to flow through the network. Firms can protect against identity theft by using assistance from advisory sources such as the Identity Theft Resource Center and by implementing the identity-theft protection provisions of the federal FACTA rule for maintaining and destroying personal information records. To combat viruses, worms, and Trojan horses, *anti-virus software* products search incoming email and data files for "signatures" of known viruses and virus-like characteristics. Contaminated files are discarded or placed in quarantine for safe-keeping. Additional intrusion protection is available by installing *anti-spyware* and *spam filtering software*.

Critical Thinking Questions—Answers

1. **Explain how data conferencing is used to save time and money.**
   Data conferencing allows people in remote locations to work simultaneously on one document.

2. **How has information technology (IT) contributed to greater organizational efficiency?**
   Networks and technology have lead to leaner companies with fewer employees and simpler structures. Networks enable firms to maintain information linkages among both employees and customers so that more work and greater customer satisfaction can be accomplished with fewer people.

Brain Teaser—Answer

Describe how managers use data mining.

Data mining helps managers plan for new products, set prices, and identify trends and shopping patterns.

Chapter 14
The Role of Accountants and Accounting Information

Learning Objectives
After reading this chapter, you should be able to:

1. Explain the role of accountants and distinguish between the kinds of work done by public accountants, private accountants, management accountants, and forensic accountants.
2. Explain how the accounting equation is used.
3. Describe the three basic financial statements and show how they reflect the activity and financial condition of a business.
4. Explain the key standards and principles for reporting financial statements.
5. Describe how computing financial ratios can help users get more information from financial statements to determine the financial strengths of a business.
6. Discuss the role of ethics in accounting.

True-False
Indicate whether the statement is generally true or false by placing a "T" or an "F" in the space provided. If it is a false statement, correct it so that it becomes a true statement.

_____ 1. Accounting is important to business because it helps managers plan and control a company's operation; and it helps outsiders evaluate a business.

_____ 2. Bookkeeping is the same as accounting.

_____ 3. Managerial accounting is the area of accounting concerned with preparing financial information for users outside the organization.

_____ 4. Certified public accountants (CPAs) are professionally licensed by the state and offer services to the public.

_____ 5. Generally accepted accounting principles (GAAP) are professionally approved standards and practices used by the accountants in the preparation of financial reports.

_____ 6. The internal auditor is the highest-ranking accountant in a company.

_____ 7. Private accountants are independent of the businesses, organizations, and individuals they serve.

_____ 8.   The CPA Vision Project developed recommendations for change, including a set of core services that the accounting profession should offer clients, and a set of core competencies that CPAs should possess.

_____ 9.   Assets = Liabilities – Owners' Equity is the basic accounting equation.

_____ 10. Owners' equity is any economic resource expected to benefit a firm or an individual who owns it.

_____ 11. Owners' equity consists of two sources of capital: the amount that the owners originally invested and the profits earned by and reinvested in the company.

_____ 12. Double-entry bookkeeping is a system of recording financial transactions to keep the accounting equation in balance.

_____ 13. Three broad categories of financial statements are balance sheets, income statements, and statements of cash flow.

_____ 14. The income statement provides a snapshot of the business at a particular time, whereas the balance sheet reflects the results of operations over a period of time.

_____ 15. Profit = Revenues – Expenses

_____ 16. Retained earnings are earnings not distributed to owners in the form of dividends.

_____ 17. The Certified Fraud Examiner (CFE) designation is earned once the requirements for the CPA are met.

_____ 18. The statement of cash flows describes yearly cash receipts and cash payments.

_____ 19. Various ratios measure solvency (a firm's ability to pay its debt) in both the short and long run.

_____ 20. Return on investment and earnings per share measure profitability.

_____ 21. Forensic accounting is known as "the private eyes of the corporate culture" because it uses accounting for legal purposes.

Multiple Choice

Circle the best answer for each of the following questions.

1. Accounting information
   a. helps managers make business decisions and spot problems and opportunities.
   b. provides investors, suppliers, and creditors with the means to analyze a business.
   c. supports the government's efforts to collect taxes and regulate business.
   d. All of the above.

2. Which of the following statements is *true*?
   a. Bookkeeping is the record-keeping, clerical phase of accounting.
   b. The controller is a person who manages all of a firm's accounting activities.
   c. Financial accounting is the field of accounting concerned with external users of a company's financial information.
   d. All of the above.

3. The area of accounting concerned with preparing data for use by managers within the organization is
   a. financial accounting.   b. managerial accounting.
   c. public accounting.   d. tax accounting.

4. Which of the following statements is *true*?
   a. An audit is a systematic examination of a company's accounting system to determine whether its financial reports fairly represent its operations.
   b. A public accountant is a salaried accountant hired by a business to carry out its day-to-day financial activities.
   c. There is little need for the accounting profession to change.
   d. All of the above.

5. In the accounting equation,
   a. Assets = Liabilities + Owners' Equity.
   b. assets are a claim against a firm by a creditor.
   c. liabilities are anything of value owned or leased by a company.
   d. All of the above.

6. Which of the following statements is *true*?
   a. Borrowing funds gives a firm leverage, the ability to make otherwise unaffordable investments.
   b. A balance sheet is a financial statement showing a firm's assets, liabilities, and owners' equity.
   c. Liquidity is the ease with which an asset can be converted into cash.
   d. All of the above.

7. Which of the following statements is *false*?
    a. Depreciation is an accounting procedure for systematically spreading the cost of an asset over its estimated useful life.
    b. A liability is anything of value owned or leased by a company.
    c. Accounts receivable is the amount due from a customer who has purchased goods on credit.
    d. Merchandise inventory is the cost of merchandise that has been acquired for sale to customers and is still on hand.

8. Which of the following statements is *false*?
    a. A fixed asset is an asset with long-term use or value, such as land, buildings, and equipment.
    b. An intangible asset is a nonphysical asset, such as a patent or trademark, that has economic value in the form of expected benefits.
    c. Current liability is debt that is not due for more than 1 year.
    d. Goodwill is the amount paid for an existing business above the value of its other assets.

9. Current liabilities consisting of bills owed to suppliers, plus wages and taxes due within the upcoming year, is
    a. long-term liability.
    b. accounts receivable.
    c. accounts payable.
    d. an intangible asset.

10. A statement of a firm's financial position on a particular date, also known as a statement of financial position, is
    a. a balance sheet.
    b. an income statement.
    c. a statement of cash flows.
    d. a cost of goods sold statement.

11. The balance sheet
    a. "balances" because it includes all elements in the accounting equation and shows the balance between assets on one side of the equation and liabilities and owners' equity on the other side.
    b. shows how profitable the organization has been over a specific period of time, typically 1 year.
    c. unfortunately does not enable the reader to determine the size of the company nor what the major assets, liabilities, or owners' equity is.
    d. All of the above.

12. Which of the following statements is *false*?
    a. Retained earnings are earnings retained by a firm for its use rather than paid as dividends.
    b. Net Income = Gross Profit – Operating Expenses and Income Taxes.
    c. Operating expenses are the amount of funds that flow into a business from the sale of goods and services.
    d. Gross profit is the amount remaining when the cost of goods sold is deducted from revenues.

13. Which of the following statements is *false*?
    a. A budget is the detailed statement of estimated receipts and expenditures for a period of time in the future.
    b. An income statement is a financial statement listing a firm's annual revenues and expenses so that a bottom line shows an annual profit or loss.
    c. The segments of an income statement are assets, liabilities, and owners' equity.
    d. The statement of cash flows shows how cash was received and spent in three areas: operations, investments, and financing.

14. Financial ratios, either short- or long-term, for estimating the risk in investing in a firm, are
    a. liquidity ratios.   b. solvency ratios.
    c. activity ratios.   d. profitability ratios.

15. Investigating a trail of financial transactions behind a suspected crime, such as money laundering or an investment swindle, would most closely be associated with
    a. private accounting.   b. investigative accounting.
    c. management accounting.   d. public accounting.

16. The accountant who can provide competent advice for strategic action by combining data, knowledge, and insight is using
    a. leadership skills.   b. communication skills.
    c. technology skills.   d. critical thinking skills.

Match the Terms and Concepts with Their Definitions

a. accounting
b. bookkeeping
c. information (AIS)
d. controller
e. financial accounting
f. managerial (or management) accounting

g. certified public accountant
h. audit
i. generally accepted accounting principles (GAAP)
j. management advisory services
k. private accountant
l. asset
m. liability
n. owners' equity
o. CPA Vision Project
p. financial statement
q. balance sheet
r. current asset

s. liquidity
t. cost of revenues
u. revenue recognition
v. Sarbanes-Oxley Act
w. fixed asset
x. depreciation
y. intangible asset

z. goodwill
aa. current liability
bb. accounts payable
cc. long-term liability
dd. paid-in capital
ee. retained earnings
ff. income statement (or profit-and-loss statement)
gg. revenues
hh. cost of goods sold
ii. gross profit
jj. operating expenses
kk. operating income

ll. net income
mm. statement of cash flows
nn. budget
oo. solvency ratio
pp. profitability ratio
qq. activity ratio
rr. certified management accountant (CMA)
ss. current ratio
tt. management accountant
uu. forensic accounting
vv. tax services
ww. certified fraud examiner
xx. audit
yy. debt
zz. leverage
aaa. AICPA
bbb. ethics
ccc. earnings per share

_____ 1.   A financial statement describing a firm's yearly cash receipts and cash payments.

_____ 2.   The costs that a company incurs to obtain revenues from other companies.

_____ 3.   A financial statement listing a firm's annual revenues and expenses so that a bottom line shows annual profit or loss.

_____ 4.   The recording of accounting transactions.

_____ 5.   A process of distributing the cost of an asset over its life.

_____ 6.   Maintains and enforces the code of professional conduct.

_____ 7.   A private accountant who provides financial services to support managers in various business activities within a firm.

_____ 8.   A systematic examination of a company's accounting system to determine whether its financial reports fairly represent its operations.

_____ 9.   A detailed statement of estimated receipts and expenditures in the future.

_____ 10. Debt that must be paid within the year.

_____ 11. Debt owned by a firm to an outside organization or individual.

_____ 12. A person who manages all of a firm's accounting activities (chief accounting officer).

_____ 13. The examination of a company's accounting information system to determine if financial reports reliably represent its operations.

_____ 14. The professional designation awarded by the Institute of Management Accountants in recognition of management accounting qualifications.

_____ 15. A financial statement detailing a firm's assets, liabilities, and owners' equity.

_____ 16. A salaried accountant hired by a business to carry out its day-to-day financial activities.

_____ 17. Field of accounting that serves internal users of a company's financial information.

_____ 18. Costs, other than the cost of goods sold, incurred in producing a good or service.

_____ 19. Debt that is not due for more than 1 year.

_____ 20. Means doing the right thing.

_____ 21. Identifies core competencies for accounting.

_____ 22. Assistance provided by CPAs for tax preparation and tax planning.

_____ 23. The accepted rules and procedures governing the content and form of financial reports.

_____ 24. The financial ratio used for evaluating management's use of a firm's assets.

_____ 25. The funds that flow into a business from the sale of goods or services.

_____ 26. Any of several types of reports summarizing a company's financial status to aid in managerial decision making.

_____ 27. A firm's total liabilities.

_____ 28. The amount paid for an existing business above the value of its other assets.

_____ 29. The organized means by which financial information is identified, measured, recorded, and retained for use in accounting statements and management reports.

_____ 30. The total cost of obtaining materials for making products sold by a firm during the year.

_____ 31. Enacted as a direct response to widely publicized financial abuses and to restore public trust in corporate accounting practices.

_____ 32. The comprehensive system for collecting, analyzing, and communicating financial information.

_____ 33. An asset that can or will be converted into cash within the following year.

_____ 34. The "private eyes of the corporate culture."

_____ 35. The earnings retained by a firm for its use rather than paid as dividends.

_____ 36. Gross profit minus operating expenses and income taxes.

_____ 37. The financial ratio used for measuring a firm's potential earnings.

_____ 38. The field of accounting concerned with external users of a company's financial information.

_____ 39. The amount of money that owners would receive if they sold all of a firm's assets and paid all of its liabilities.

_____ 40. The ability to finance an investment through borrowed funds.

_____ 41. An asset with long-term use or value, such as land, buildings, and equipment.

_____ 42. Current liabilities consisting of bills owed to suppliers, plus wages and taxes due within the upcoming year.

_____ 43. A profitability ratio measuring the size of the dividend that a firm can pay shareholders.

_____ 44. An accountant licensed by the state and offering services to the public.

_____ 45. The solvency ratio that determines a firm's credit worthiness by measuring its ability to pay current liabilities.

_____ 46. Specialized accounting services to help managers resolve many business problems.

_____ 47. Any economic resource expected to benefit a firm or an individual who owns it.

_____ 48. A nonphysical asset, such as a patent or trademark, that has economic value in the form of expected benefit.

_____ 49. Designated to work in the specialty area of forensic accounting focusing on fraud-related issues.

_____ 50. The financial ratio, either short- or long-term, used for estimating risks in investing in a firm.

_____ 51. A formal recording and reporting of revenues at the appropriate time.

_____ 52. The revenues obtained from goods sold, minus cost of goods sold.

_____ 53. The ease with which an asset can be converted into cash.

_____ 54. Additional money, above proceeds from stock sale, paid directly to a firm by its owners.

_____ 55. Gross profit minus operating expenses.

Jeopardy

Accountants and the Systems They Manage	Does It Balance?	Know Your Ratios
1. Accounting system concerned with external users What is _____?	1. Things you own What are _____?	1. Difference between a firm's current assets and current liabilities What is _____?
2. Licensed accountants Who are _____?	2. Things you owe What are _____?	2. Used to calculate a firm's creditworthiness What is the _____?
3. Accounting system concerned with internal users What is _____?	3. Assets – Liabilities What is _____?	3. Determines the size of dividends that a firm can pay What is _____?

Pick the Correct Word

Circle the best word or phrase for each sentence.

1. (Forensic) (Managerial) accountants use accounting for legal purposes by providing investigative and litigation support in crimes.

2. To ensure integrity in reporting, CPAs are always (dependent) (independent) of the firms they audit.

3. (Assets) (Inventories) include land, buildings, equipment, inventory, and accounts receivable due the company.

4. If a company's assets exceed its liabilities, owners' equity is (positive) (negative); if liabilities outweigh assets, owners' equity is (positive) (negative); assets are insufficient to pay off all debts.

5. (Short-term) (Long-term) liabilities represent borrowed funds on which the company must pay interest.

6. Although the (accounting) (marketing) staff coordinates the budget process, it needs input from many areas regarding proposed activities and required resources.

7. When a company operates profitably, its assets (increase) (decrease) faster than its liabilities.

8. (Income statements) (Balance sheets) are sometimes called statements of financial position.

9. Accounts (receivable) (payable) are amounts due from customers who have goods on credit.

10. (Current) (Long-term) assets include cash and assets that can be converted into cash within a year.

Learning Objectives—Short Answer or Essay Questions

Learning Objective #1: Explain the role of accountants and distinguish between the kinds of work done by public accountants, private accountants, management accountants, and forensic accountants.

Learning Objective #2: Explain how the accounting equation is used.

Learning Objective #3: Describe the three basic financial statements and show how they reflect the activity and financial condition of a business.

Learning Objective #4: Explain the key standards and principles for reporting financial statements.

Learning Objective #5 Describe how computing financial ratios can help users get more information from financial statements to determine the financial strengths of a business.

Learning Objective #6: Discuss the role of ethics in accounting.

Critical Thinking Question

Use the accounts below to answer the following questions:

Net sales	Accounts receivable	Advertising expense
Common stock	Equipment	Marketable securities
Salaries	Retained earnings	Long-term notes payable
Cash	Inventory	Rent

    a.   Which of these would be considered a current asset? Why?

    b.   Which of these would be considered a fixed asset? Why?

    c.   Which of these would be considered a current liability? Why?

    d.   Which of these would be considered a long-term liability? Why?

    e.   Which of these would be considered owners' equity?

    f.   Which of these would be considered revenue?

    g.   Which of these would be considered an expense?

Brain Treaser

At the end of the year, Jan Nord, Inc., showed the following balances on accounts.
Prepare a balance sheet for Jan Nord, Inc.

Land	$70,000
Buildings	320,000
Inventory	110,000
Cash	20,000
Accounts payable	120,000
Marketable securities	42,000
Retained earnings	392,000
Common shares	80,000
(40,000 share @ $2)	
Notes payable	120,000
Equipment	60,000

ANSWERS

True-False—Answers

1. True
2. False: Bookkeeping, which is sometimes confused with accounting, *is just one phase of accounting*—the recording of accounting transactions.
3. False: *Financial accounting* is the area of accounting concerned with preparing financial information for users outside the organization.
4. True
5. True
6. False: The *controller* is the highest-ranking accountant in a company.
7. False: *Public accountants* are independent of the businesses, organizations, and individuals they serve.
8. True
9. False: Assets = Liabilities + Owners' Equity is the basic accounting equation.
10. False: An *asset* is any economic resource expected to benefit a firm or an individual who owns it.
11. True
12. True
13. True
14. False: The *balance sheet* provides a snapshot of the business at a particular time, whereas the *income statement* reflects the results of operations over a period of time.
15. True
16. True
17. False: The Certified Fraud Examiner (CFE) designation is a specific specialty area within forensic accounting. It s administered by Association of Certified Fraud Examiners and focuses specifically on fraud-related issues
18. True
19. True
20. True
21. True

Multiple Choice—Answers

1. d	5. a	9. c	13. c
2. d	6. d	10. a	14. b
3. b	7. b	11. a	15. b
4. a	8. c	12. c	16. d

Match the Terms and Concepts with Their Definitions—Answers

1. mm	9. nn	17. f	25. gg	33. r	41. w	49. ww
2. t	10. aa	18. jj	26. p	34. uu	42. bb	50. oo
3. ff	11. m	19. cc	27. yy	35. ee	43. ccc	51. u
4. b	12. d	20. bbb	28. z	36. ll	44. g	52. ii
5. x	13. xx	21. o	29. c	37. pp	45. ss	53. s
6. aaa	14. rr	22. vv	30. hh	38. e	46. j	54. dd
7. tt	15. q	23. i	31. v	39. n	47. l	55. kk
8. h	16. k	24. qq	32. a	40. zz	48. y	

Jeopardy—Answers

Accounting Systems and Accountants	Does It Balance?	Know Your Ratios
1. What is financial accounting?	1. What are assets?	1. What is working capital?
2. Who are CPAs?	2. What are liabilities?	2. What is the current ratio?
3. What is managerial accounting?	3. What is owners' equity?	3. What is earnings per share?

Pick the Correct Word—Answers

1. Forensic
2. independent
3. assets
4. positive, negative
5. Long-term

6. accounting
7. increase
8. Balance sheets
9. receivable
10. Current

Learning Objectives—Short Answer or Essay Questions—Answers

Learning Objective #1: Explain the role of accountants and distinguish between the kinds of work done by public accountants, private accountants, management accountants, and forensic accountants.
By collecting, analyzing, and communicating financial information, accountants provide business managers and investors with an accurate picture of the firm's financial health. *Certified public accountants (CPAs)* are licensed professionals who provide auditing, tax, and management advisory services for other firms and individuals. *Public accountants* have not yet been certified perform similar tasks. *Private accountants* provide diverse specialized services for the specific firms that employ them. Most private accountants are *management accountants* who provide services to support managers in various activities such as marketing, production, and engineering. They may hold the certified management

accountant (CMA) designation. *Forensic accountants* are detectives looking behind the corporate façade instead of accepting financial records at face value.

Learning Objective #2: Explain how the accounting equation is used.

Accountants use the following equation to balance the data pertaining to financial transactions: Assets – Liabilities = Owners' Equity. After each financial transaction (e.g., payments to suppliers, sales to customers, wages to employees), the accounting equation must be in balance. If it isn't, then an accounting error has occurred. The equation also provides an indication of the firm's financial health. If assets exceed liabilities, owners' equity is positive; if the firm goes out of business, owners will receive some cash (a gain) after selling assets and paying off liabilities. If liabilities outweigh assets, owners' equity is negative; assets aren't enough to pay off debts. If the company goes under, owners will get no cash and some creditors won't be paid, thus, losing their remaining investments in the company.

Learning Objective #3: Describe the three basic financial statements and show how they reflect the activity and financial condition of a business.

(1) The *balance sheet* (sometimes called the *statement of financial position*) supplies detailed information about the accounting equation factors—assets, liabilities, and owners' equity—that together are a barometer of the firm's financial condition at a given point in time. By comparing the current balance sheet with those of previous years, creditors and owners can better interpret the firm's financial progress and future prospects. (2) The *income statement* (sometimes called a *profit-and-loss statement*) describes revenues and expenses to show a firm's annual profit or loss during a period of time, such as a year. (3) A publicly traded firm must issue a *statement of cash flows*, which describes its yearly cash receipts (inflows) and payments (outflows). It shows the effects on cash during the year from three kinds of business activities: (a) cash flows from operations, (b) cash flows from investing, and (c) cash flows from financing. The statement of cash flows then reports the overall change in the company's cash position at the end of the accounting period.

Learning Objective #4: Explain the key standards and principles for reporting financial statements.

Accountants follow standard reporting practices and principles when preparing external reports. The common language dictated by standard practices is designed to give external users confidence in the accuracy and meaning of financial information. Spelled out in GAAP, these principles cover a range of issues, such as when to recognize revenues from operations and how to make full public disclosure of financial information. Without such standards, users of financial statements wouldn't be able to compare information from different companies, and thus they would misunderstand—or be led to misconstrue—a company's true financial status.

Learning Objective #5: Describe how computing financial ratios can help users get more information from financial statements to determine the financial strengths of a business.

Drawing on data from financial statements, ratios help creditors, investors, and managers assess a firm's finances. Statements provide data, which can in turn reveal trends and can be applied to various ratios. We use these ratios to evaluate a firm's financial health, its progress, and its prospects for the future.

Ratios are normally grouped into three major classifications:
* Solvency ratios for estimating short-term and long-term risk
* Profitability ratios for measuring potential earnings
* Activity ratios for evaluating management's use of assets

Learning Objective #6: Discuss the role of ethics in accounting.

The purpose of ethics in accounting is to maintain public confidence in business institutions, financial markets, and the products and services of the accounting profession. Without ethics, all of accounting's tools and methods would be meaningless because their usefulness depends, ultimately, on veracity in their application.

Critical Thinking Question—Answers

Use the accounts below to answer the following questions:

Net sales	Accounts receivable	Advertising expense
Common stock	Equipment	Marketable securities
Salaries	Retained earnings	Long-term notes payable
Cash	Inventory	Rent

   a. Cash, accounts receivable, inventory, and marketable securities would all be considered current assets.
   b. Equipment is the only fixed asset on this list.
   c. Salaries, advertising expenses, and rent accrued are the current liabilities.
   d. Long-term notes payable are the only long-term liability on this list.
   e. Common stock and retained earnings are the owners' equity.
   f. Net sales and interest from marketable securities (and retained earnings if it is earning interest) constitute revenue.
   g. Expenses include salaries, advertising expenses, interest on long-term notes payable, and rent (as well as depreciation on the equipment).

Brain Teaser—Answer

Jan Nord, Inc.
Balance Sheet

ASSETS

Current Assets

Cash	$110,000	
Marketable Securities	42,000	
Inventory	110,000	
Total Current Assets	$262,000	

Fixed Assets

Land	$70,000	
Buildings	320,000	
Equipment	60,000	
Total Fixed Assets	$450,000	
Total Assets		**$712,000**

LIABILITIES AND OWNERS' EQUITY

Current Liabilities

Accounts Payable	$120,000	
Total Current Liabilities	120,000	

Long-Term Liabilities

Notes Payable	$120,000	
Total Long-Term Liabilities	$120,000	
Total Liabilities		**$240,000**

Owners' Equity

Common Shares	$80,000	
(40,000 shares @ $2)		
Retained Earnings	$392,000	
Total Owners' Equity		**$472,000**
Total Liabilities & Owners' Equity		**$712,000**

Chapter 15
Money and Banking

Learning Objectives
After reading this chapter, you should be able to:

1. Define *money* and identify the different forms that it takes in the nation's money supply.
2. Describe the different kinds of financial institutions that comprise the U.S. financial system and explain the services they offer.
3. Explain how financial institutions create money and describe the means by which they are regulated.
4. Discuss the functions of the Federal Reserve System and describe the tools that it uses to control the money supply.
5. Identify three important ways in which the money and banking system is changing.
6. Discuss some of the institutions and activities in international banking and finance.

True-False
Indicate whether the statement is generally true or false by placing a "T" or an "F" in the space provided. If it is a false statement, correct it so that it becomes a true statement.

_____ 1. Anything that is going to be money must be portable, divisible, durable, and stable.

_____ 2. Money serves three functions: it acts as a medium of exchange, a store of value, and a unit of account.

_____ 3. M-2 is a measure of the money supply that includes only the most liquid (spendable) forms of money.

_____ 4. The major components of M-2 are M-1, time deposits, money market mutual funds, and savings deposits.

_____ 5. A demand deposit is a collection of short-term, low-risk financial securities.

_____ 6. Some of the major types of financial institutions that accept deposits from the general public include commercial banks, savings and loan associations, mutual savings banks, and credit unions.

_____ 7. The prime rate is the interest rate available to a bank's most credit-worthy customers.

_____ 8. The Federal Reserve System (the Fed) is the nation's central bank.

_____ 9. Banks create money (add to the money supply) whenever loans are repaid.

_____ 10. The Federal Deposit Insurance Corporation (FDIC) is the primary agency responsible for ensuring a sound, competitive, financial system.

_____ 11. The Fed's most important function is to control the nation's money supply.

_____ 12. To change the money supply and interest rates, the Fed can change reserve requirements, the discount rate, and utilize open market operations.

_____ 13. To increase the money supply, the Fed should increase the discount rate.

_____ 14. To increase the money supply, the Fed should increase the reserve requirement.

_____ 15. When the Federal Reserve sets margin requirements for consumer stock purchases or sets credit rules for other consumer purchases, it's exercising selective credit controls.

_____ 16. Deregulation of the banking business and interest rates, as well as the rise of interstate banking, has increased competition in the banking business.

_____ 17. A smart card is a card that allows an individual to transfer money between accounts.

_____ 18. E-cash is money that can be moved among consumers and businesses via digital electronic transmission.

_____ 19. Each nation tries to influence its currency exchange rates to gain advantage in international trade.

_____ 20. A higher exchange rate usually results in a nation having a greater trade surplus.

Multiple Choice

Circle the best answer for each of the following questions.

1. Money functions as a
   a. medium of exchange.   b. unit of value.
   c. store of value.   d. All of the above.

2. Money must be
   a. divisible.   b. portable.
   c. durable and stable.   d. All of the above.

3. Which of the following statements is *true*?
   a. M-2 counts only the most liquid, or spendable, forms of money: currency, demand deposits, or low-interest-bearing forms of money.
   b. The major components of M-2 are M-1, time deposits, money market mutual funds, and savings deposits.
   c. Time deposits are bank account funds that may be withdrawn at any time by simply writing a check.
   d. All of the above.

4. Which of the following statements is *true* about credit cards?
   a. Credit cards are extremely profitable for issuing companies.
   b. Merchants who accept credit cards pay fees to card issuers.
   c. All credit cards charge interest on unpaid balances; some charge an annual fee to card holders.
   d. All of the above.

5. Which of the following are nondeposit financial institutions?
   a. Commercial banks   b. Savings and loan associations
   c. Insurance companies   d. Credit unions

6. A financial institution that only accepts deposits from, and makes loans to, its members, usually employees of a particular organization, is a
   a. credit union.   b. commercial bank.
   c. savings and loan association.   d. mutual savings bank.

7. A nondeposit financial institution that specializes in making loans to businesses and consumers is
   a. an insurance company.   b. a finance company.
   c. a securities investment dealer.   d. a pension fund.

8. A nondeposit financial institution that pools funds managed to provide retirement income for its members is
   a. an insurance company.   b. a securities investment dealer.
   c. a pension fund.   d. a finance company.

9. A tax-deferred pension fund with which wage earners supplement other retirement funds is

    a. a trust service.

    b. a letter of credit.

    c. an individual retirement account.

    d. a banker's acceptance.

10. Which of the following statements is *true*?

    a. When banks make loans, the money supply increases.

    b. The Federal Deposit Insurance Corporation (FDIC) is a federal agency that guarantees the safety of all deposits up to $100,000 in the financial institutions that it insures.

    c. Because commercial banks are critical to the creation of money, the government regulates them to ensure a sound and competitive financial system.

    d. All of the above.

11. The Federal Reserve System (the Fed)

    a. acts as the government's bank.

    b. can lend money to member commercial banks.

    c. controls the nation's money supply.

    d. All of the above.

12. Which of the following statements is *false*?

    a. The Fed, as the bankers' bank, lends money (at interest) to member banks, stores required reserve funds for banks, and clears checks for them.

    b. The Fed does not have the power to audit banks.

    c. The Fed lends money to the government whenever it buys bonds issued by the Treasury Department.

    d. The Fed controls monetary policy—the management of the nation's money supply and interest rates.

13. Which of the following statements is *false* about the Fed's monetary policy tools?

    a. The discount rate is the interest rate that a bank charges its most creditworthy customers for consumer loans.

    b. Open market operations are the Fed's sales and purchases of government securities in the open market.

    c. The reserve requirement is the percentage of banks' deposits that must be held in cash or on deposit with the Federal Reserve.

    d. The Federal Reserve can use selective credit controls to set margin requirements governing the credit granted to buyers of securities.

14. To increase the money supply, the Fed could

    a. reduce the discount rate.

    b. reduce reserve requirements.

    c. buy U.S. Treasury notes and bonds on the open market.

    d. All of the above.

15. Which of the following is *true*?
    a. A smart card is a card that allows someone to transfer money between bank accounts.
    b. A debit card is a credit-card-sized computer programmed with electronic money.
    c. A point-of-sale (POS) terminal is an electronic device that allows customers to pay for retail purchases with debit cards.
    d. All of the above.

16. If the value of the U.S. dollar in international exchange markets increases (the dollar appreciates, it gets stronger) this will likely cause
    a. the relative price of American products to become more expensive and the U.S. will export less.
    b. the relative price of foreign products to become less expensive and the U.S. will import more.
    c. a trade deficit in the United States.
    d. All of the above.

17. The International Monetary Fund attempts to
    a. promote stable exchange rates.
    b. provide temporary, short-term loans to member countries.
    c. encourage members to cooperate on international monetary issues.
    d. All of the above.

Match the Terms and Concepts with Their Definitions

a. money

b. M-1

c. currency

d. check

e. M-2

f. time deposit

g. money market mutual fund

h. commercial bank

i. demand deposit

j. World Bank

k. prime rate

l. savings and loan association (S&L)

m. mutual savings bank

n. credit union

o. pension fund

p. insurance company

q. finance company

r. securities investment dealer (broker)

s. individual retirement account (IRA)

t. International Monetary Fund (IMF)

u. trust services

v. letter of credit

w. banker's acceptance

x. automated teller machine

y. electronic funds transfer (EFT)

z. Federal Deposit Insurance Corporation (FDIC)

aa. Federal Reserve System (the Fed)

bb. mutual savings bank

cc. monetary policy

dd. reserve requirement

ee. discount rate

ff. open-market operations

gg. banker's acceptance

hh. debit card

ii. point-of-sale (POS) terminal

jj. smart card

kk. E-cash

_____ 1. A demand deposit order instructing a bank to pay a given sum to a specified payee.

_____ 2. A financial institution accepting deposits and making loans primarily for home mortgages.

_____ 3. The interest rate at which member banks can borrow money from the Federal Reserve.

_____ 4. The communication of fund-transfer information over wire, cable, or microwave.

_____ 5. A federal- or state-chartered financial institution accepting deposits that it uses to make loans and earn profits.

_____ 6. A credit-card-size computer programmed with electronic money.

_____ 7. A nondeposit institution that buys and sells stocks and bonds, both for investors and for its own accounts.

_____ 8. A bank promise, issued for a buyer, to pay a designated firm a certain amount of money if specified conditions are met.

_____ 9. A financial institution that accepts deposits from, and makes loans to, only its members, usually employees of a particular organization.

_____ 10. A plastic card that allows an individual to transfer money between accounts.

_____ 11. The central bank of the United States, which acts as the government's bank, serves member commercial banks, and controls the nation's money supply.

_____ 12. A bank funds that cannot be withdrawn without notice or transferred by check.

_____ 13. A nondeposit institution that invests funds collected as premiums charged for insurance coverage.

_____ 14. Any object that is portable, divisible, durable, and stable, and serves as a medium of exchange, a store of value, and a unit of account.

_____ 15. Bank account funds that may be withdrawn at any time.

_____ 16. The policies by which the Federal Reserve manages the nation's money supply and interest rates.

_____ 17. A bank promise, issued for a buyer, to pay a designated firm a specified amount at a future date.

_____ 18. Government-issued paper money and metal coins.

_____ 19. A nondeposit pool of funds managed to provide retirement income for its members.

_____ 20. A bank promise, issued for a buyer, to pay a designated firm a specified amount at a future date.

_____ 21. The federal agency that guarantees the safety of all deposits up to $100,000 in the financial institutions that it insures.

_____ 22. The United Nations agency consisting of about 150 nations that have combined resources to promote stable exchange rates, provide temporary short-term loans, and serve other purposes.

_____ 23. The measure of the money supply that includes all the components of M-1, plus the forms of money that can be easily converted into spendable form.

_____ 24. The interest rate available to a bank's most creditworthy customers.

_____ 25. A financial institution whose depositors are owners sharing in its profits.

_____ 26. A fund of short-term, low-risk financial securities purchased with the assets of investor-owners, pooled by a nonbank institution.

_____ 27. An electronic device that allows customers to pay for retail purchases with debit cards.

_____ 28. An electronic machine that allows customers to conduct account-related activities 24 hours a day, 7 days a week.

_____ 29. Electronic money that moves among consumers and businesses via digital electronic transmissions.

_____ 30. A financial institution whose depositors are owners sharing in its profits.

_____ 31. A tax-deferred pension fund with which wage earners supplement other retirement funds.

_____ 32. A nondeposit institution that specializes in making loans to businesses and consumers.

_____ 33. The measure of the money supply that includes only the most liquid (spendable) form of money.

_____ 34. The percentage of its deposits that a bank must hold in cash or on deposit with the Federal Reserve.

_____ 35. The United Nations agency that provides a limited scope of financial services, such as funding national improvements in undeveloped countries.

_____ 36. Bank management of an individual's investments, payments, or estate.

_____ 37. The Federal Reserve's sales and purchases of securities in the open market.

Let's List
Answer the following questions with a series of lists:

1. What are four characteristics of money?
   a. _____
   b. _____
   c. _____
   d. _____

2. List three functions of money.
   a. _____
   b. _____
   c. _____
   d. _____

3. List four types of nondeposit institutions.
   a. _____
   b. _____
   c. _____
   d. _____

4. List three international services that can be offered by a bank.
   a. _____
   b. _____
   c. _____

5. List four functions of the International Monetary Fund.
   a. _____
   b. _____
   c. _____
   d. _____

Learning Objectives –Short Answer or Essay Questions

Learning Objective #1: Define *money* and identify the different forms it takes in the nation's money supply.

Learning Objective #2: Describe the different kinds of financial institutions that comprise the U.S. financial system and explain the services they offer.

Learning Objective #3: Explain how financial institutions create money and describe the means by which they are regulated.

Learning Objective #4: Discuss the functions of the Federal Reserve System and describe the tools it uses to control the money supply.

Learning Objective #5: Identify three important ways in which the money and banking system is changing.

Learning Objective #6: Discuss some of the institutions and activities in international banking and finance.

Critical Thinking Questions

1. Why is it necessary for the government to regulate commercial banks?

2. How can the Federal Reserve decrease the money supply?

Brain Teaser

How can an increase in the money supply stimulate the economy?

ANSWERS

True-False—Answers

1. True
2. True
3. False: *M-1* is a measure of the money supply that includes only the most liquid (spendable) forms of money.
4. True
5. False: A *money market mutual fund* is a collection of short-term, low-risk financial securities.
6. True
7. True
8. True
9. False: Banks create money (add to the supply) whenever loans are *made* (or granted).
10. True
11. True
12. True
13. False: To increase the money supply, the Fed should *decrease* the discount rate.
14. False: To increase the money supply, the Fed should *decrease* the reserve requirement.
15. True
16. True
17. False: A *debit* card is a card that allows an individual to transfer money between accounts.
18. True
19. True
20. False: A higher exchange rate results in a nation experiencing a greater trade *deficit*.

Multiple Choice—Answers

1. d	5. c	9. c	13. a	17. d
2. d	6. a	10. d	14. d	
3. b	7. b	11. d	15. c	
4. d	8. c	12. b	16. d	

Match the Terms and Concepts with Their Definitions—Answers

1. d	6. jj	11. aa	16. cc	21. z	26. g	31. s	36. u
2. l	7. r	12. f	17. w	22. t	27. ii	32. q	37. ff
3. ee	8. v	13. p	18. c	23. e	28. x	33. b	
4. y	9. n	14. a	19. o	24. k	29. kk	34. dd	
5. h	10. hh	15. i	20. gg	25. bb	30. m	35. j	

Let's List—Answers

1. What are four characteristics of money?
   a. portability
   b. divisibility
   c. durability
   d. stability

2. List three functions of money.
   a. medium of exchange
   b. store of value
   c. unit of account

3. List four types of nondeposit institutions.
   a. pension funds
   b. insurance companies
   c. finance companies
   d. securities dealers

4. List three international services that can be offered by a bank.
   a. Currency Exchange
   b. Letters of Credit
   c. Banker's Acceptance

5. List four functions of the International Monetary Fund.
   a. To promote the stability of exchange rates
   b. To provide temporary, short-term loans to member countries
   c. To encourage members to cooperate on international monetary issues
   d. To encourage development of a system for international payments

Learning Objectives—Short Answer or Essay Questions—Answers

Learning Objective #1: Define *money* and identify the different forms that it takes in the nation's money supply.

Any item that is portable, divisible, durable, and stable satisfies the four basic characteristics of *money*. Money also serves three functions: it is a medium of exchange, a store of value, and a unit of account. *The nation's money supply is usually measured in three ways. M-1* includes only the most liquid (or spendable) forms of money: currency (cash), checks, and checking accounts (demand deposits). *M-2* includes M-1 plus other forms of money that are not quite as liquid but are converted easily to spendable forms: time deposits, money market funds, and savings accounts. *M-3* includes all of M-2 plus somewhat less liquid deposits, mainly by large institutions, in large time deposits and large money market funds.

Learning Objective #2: Describe the different kinds of financial institutions that comprise the U.S. financial system and explain the services they offer.

Commercial banks offer checking accounts and accept deposits that they use to make loans and earn profits for shareholders. They also offer other services: (1) pension and trust services, (2) international services, (3) financial advice and brokerage services, (4) ATMs, and (5) other forms of electronic banking. *Savings and loan associations (S&Ls)* also accept deposits and make loans, primarily for home mortgages. In *mutual savings banks*, all depositors are owners of the bank, and all profits are divided proportionately among them. *Credit unions* are nonprofit cooperative financial institutions, owned and run by their members who pool their funds to make loans to one another at reasonable rates. Numerous other organizations called *nondeposit institutions*—pension funds, insurance companies, finance companies, and securities investment dealers—take in money, provide interest or other services, and make loans.

Learning Objective #3: Explain how financial institutions create money and describe the means by which they are regulated.

By taking in deposits and making loans, banks create money or, more accurately, *expand the money supply*. The government regulates commercial banks to ensure a sound financial system. The *Federal Deposit Insurance Corporation (FDIC)* insures deposits and guarantees the safety of all deposits up to the current maximum of $100,000. To ensure against failures, the FDIC examines the activities and accounts of all member banks.

Learning Objective #4: Discuss the functions of the Federal Reserve System and describe the tools that it uses to control the money supply.

The *Federal Reserve System (the Fed)* is the nation's central bank. As the government's bank, the Fed produces currency and lends money to the government. As the bankers' bank, it lends money (at interest) to member banks, stores required *reserve funds* for banks, and clears checks for them. The Fed is empowered to audit member banks and sets U.S. *monetary policy* by controlling the country's money supply. To control the money supply, the Fed specifies *reserve requirements* (the percentage of its deposits that a bank must hold with the Fed). It sets the *discount rate* at which it lends money to banks and conducts *open-market operations* to buy and sell securities. It also exerts influence through *selective credit controls* (such as margin requirements governing the credit granted to buyers by securities brokers).

Learning Objective #5: Identify three important ways in which the money and banking system is changing.

(1) *Anti-terrorism regulations*: The Bank Secrecy Act requires financial institutions to formulate methods to deter the funding of crimes. The USA Patriot Act is designed to reduce terrorism risks by requiring banks to implement a customer identification program to verify identities and compare them with government lists of terrorists. (2) *Interstate banking*: The Interstate Banking Efficiency Act allows banks to operate across state lines. (3) *Electronic technologies*: In addition to EFT systems, such as ATMs, banks offer telephone, TV, and Internet banking. Electronic check clearing (Check 21) speeds up the check-clearing process, and the "blink" credit card speeds up consumer checkout by replacing magnetic strip cards with contactless cards. Debit cards allow the transfer of money from the cardholder's account directly to others' accounts. The smart card can be programmed with "electronic money" at ATM machines or even at home.

Learning Objective #6: Discuss some of the institutions and activities in international banking and finance.

Because there is no worldwide banking system, global banking stability relies on a loose structure of agreements among individual countries or groups of countries. Two United Nations agencies help to finance international trade: (1) The *World Bank* funds loans for national improvements so borrowers can increase productive capacity and international trade. (2) The *International Monetary Fund (IMF)* makes loans to nations suffering from temporary negative trade balances and to provide economic and monetary stability for the borrowing country. The IMF is a group of some 150 nations that have combined resources for the following purposes:

- To promote the stability of exchange rates
- To provide temporary, short-term loans to member countries
- To encourage members to cooperate on international monetary issues
- To encourage development of a system for international payments

Critical Thinking Questions—Answers

1. **Why is it necessary for the government to regulate commercial banks?**
   Because commercial banks are essential to the creation of money, the government regulates them to ensure a sound and competitive financial system.

2. **How can the Federal Reserve decrease the money supply?**
   The Fed could decrease the money supply by increasing the discount rate, increasing reserve requirements, selling government bonds, or tightening up on select credit controls.

Brain Teaser—Answer

How can an increase in the money supply stimulate the economy?

An increase in the money supply will decrease interest rates which will stimulate borrowing and, therefore, spending. An increase in spending means more sales. More sales will stimulate production, which will increase employment and national income. A portion of the additional income earned will be spent, creating a further expansion in national employment, income, and production (GDP). The Fed should increase the money supply to fight a recession (and decrease the money supply to fight inflation during a rapidly expanding economy).

Chapter 16
Managing Finances

Learning Objectives
After reading this chapter, you should be able to:

1. Explain the concept of the time value of money and the principle of compound growth.
2. Identify the investment opportunities offered by mutual funds and exchange-traded funds.
3. Describe the role of securities markets, and identify the major stock exchanges and stock markets.
4. Explain how securities markets are regulated and tracked.
5. Describe the risk-return relationship, and discuss the use of diversification and asset allocation for investments.
6. Describe the various ways that firms raise capital and identify the pros and cons of each method.
7. Identify the reasons a company might make an initial public offering of its stock, and explain how stock value is determined.

True-False
Indicate whether the statement is generally true or false by placing a "T" or an "F" in the space provided. If it is a false statement, correct it so that it becomes a true statement.

_____ 1. The market in which new stocks and bonds are bought and sold by firms and governments is the secondary securities market.

_____ 2. Existing stocks and bonds are sold to the public in the primary securities market.

_____ 3. The shareholders of preferred stock must be paid dividends after the common stock shareholders.

_____ 4. The two different ways in which stock values are usually expressed include market value and book value.

_____ 5. Mutual funds and exchange-traded funds represent alternatives to buying stock because they offer attractive investment opportunities for various financial objectives.

_____ 6.   The current price of a share of common stock in the stock market is its book value.

_____ 7.   Default risk is the chance that one or more promised payments will be deferred or missed.

_____ 8.   Brokers at an exchange trade face-to-face on the trading floor (also referred to as an outcry market).

_____ 9.   A bond is an IOU—a promise by the issuer to pay the buyer a certain amount of money by a specified future date, usually with interest paid at regular intervals.

_____ 10. The federal government issues bonds to finance projects and meet obligations, (called municipal bonds).

_____ 11. Corporate bondholders get a fixed return and do not vote on company policy, nor do they share in company profits or losses.

_____ 12. A time period in the market when stock prices are falling is a bull market.

_____ 13. The time value of money is the principle that invested money grows, over time, by earning interest or some other form of return.

_____ 14. Corporations can raise capital by issuing bonds.

_____ 15. A bond is said to be in default if the borrower fails to make payment when due to lenders.

_____ 16. Low-grade bonds are usually called junk bonds.

_____ 17. In a secured loan for purchase of new equipment the lender does not require collateral.

_____ 18. Mutual funds pool investments from individuals and organizations to purchase a portfolio of stocks, bonds, and other securities.

Multiple Choice

Circle the best answer for each of the following questions.

1. The principle that invested money grows over time by earning interest or some other form of return is the
   a.   prospectus.   b.   time value of money.
   c.   market value.   d.   insider trading.

2. A stock's real value is its
   a.   face value.
   b.   book value.
   c.   dividend value.
   d.   market value.

3. An alternative to buying stock that often does not require large sums of money includes
   a.   mutual funds and exchange-traded funds.
   b.   dividend growth funds.
   c.   share growth funds.
   d.   stability values.

4. A prospectus is a registration statement filed with the _____ containing information for prospective investors about a security to be offered and the issuing company.
   a.   ECN
   b.   CIA
   c.   ETF
   d.   SEC

5. The market in which new stocks and bonds are bought and sold by firms and governments is the
   a.   SEC market.
   b.   discount brokers market.
   c.   primary securities market.
   d.   secondary securities market.

6. The period of rising stock prices lasting 12 months or longer featuring investor confidence for future gains and motivation to buy is a
   a.   bear market.
   b.   prime market.
   c.   bull market
   d.   All of the above.

7. NASDAQ
   a. is an acronym for the National Association of Securities Dealers Automated Quotation System.
   b. is an organization of over-the-counter dealers who own, buy, and sell their own securities over a network of electronic communications.
   c. is the fastest-growing U.S. stock market.
   d. All of the above.

8. A bond issued by a company is called a
   a. municipal bond.
   b. corporate bond.
   c. secured bond.
   d. callable bond.

9. _____ means buying several different kinds of investments rather than just one.
   a. Diversification
   b. Collateral
   c. Convertibility
   d. Capital

10. A loan for which collateral is not required is a(n)
    a. secured loan.
    b. registered bond.
    c. unsecured loan.
    d. convertible bond.

11. The first sale of a company's stock to the general public is a(n)
    a. OTC.
    b. IPO.
    c. IOU.
    d. SEC.

12. Which of the following statements is *false*?
    a. A margin is the percentage of the total sales price that a buyer must put up to place an order for stock or futures contracts.
    b. The price-earnings ratio is the current price of a stock, divided by the firm's current annual earnings per share.
    c. A bear market is a period of rising stock prices.
    d. The NASDAQ Composite Index is a value-weighted market index that includes all NASDAQ-listed companies, both domestic and foreign.

13. Outside investors who provide new capital for firms in return for a share of equity ownership are
    a. angel investors.
    b. capital gains investors.
    c. working capital investors.
    d. corporate raiders investors.

14. Long-term borrowing from sources outside a company is
    a. debt financing.
    b. equity financing.
    c. retained earnings financing.
    d. All of the above.

Match the Terms and Concepts with Their Definitions

a. securities
b. primary securities market
c. Securities and Exchange Commission (SEC)
d. investment bank
e. secondary securities market
f. portfolio
g. market value
h. stock
i. book value
j. market capitalization
k. angel investor
l. stock exchange
m. broker

n. corporate raider

o. National Association of Securities Dealers Automated Quotation (NASDAQ) System
p. collateral
q. diversification
r. municipal bond
s. corporate bond
t. default
u. securities markets
v. Russell 2000 Index
w. compound growth
x. mutual fund
y. loan principal
z. electronic communication network
aa. NASDAQ Composite Index
bb. market index

cc. bull market
dd. bear market
ee. Dow Jones Industrial Average
ff. S&P 500 Market Index

gg. common stock
hh. venture capital
ii. bond indenture
jj. interest
kk. dividend
ll. unsecured loan
mm. asset allocation
nn. prospectus

oo. insider trading
pp. time value of money

_____ 1. A bond issued by a state or local government.

_____ 2. The market index based on the performance of 400 industrial firms, 40 utilities, 40 financial institutions, and 20 transportation companies.

_____ 3. The total dollar value of all the company's outstanding shares.

_____ 4. The registration statement filed with the SEC before the issuance of a new security.

_____ 5. The federal agency that administers U.S. securities laws to protect the investing public and maintain smoothly functioning markets.

_____ 6. An investor conducting a type of hostile corporate takeover against the wishes of the company.

_____ 7. A company that pools investments from individuals and organizations to purchase a portfolio of stocks, bonds, and short-term securities.

_____ 8. The legal document containing complete details of a bond issue.

_____ 9. A loan for which collateral is not required.

_____ 10. The combined holdings of all the financial investments of any company or individual.

_____ 11. An asset pledged for the fulfillment of repaying a loan.

_____ 12. The financial institution engaged in issuing and reselling new securities.

_____ 13. The markets in which stocks and bonds are sold.

_____ 14. An organization of individuals formed to provide an institutional setting in which stock can be traded.

_____ 15. Payments to shareholders, on a per share basis, out of the company's earnings.

_____ 16. The principle that invested money grows, over time, by earning interest or some other form of return.

_____ 17. The compounding of interest over time—with each additional time period, interest returns accumulate.

_____ 18. An individual or organization who receives and executes buy-and-sell orders on behalf of other people in return for commissions.

_____ 19. A portion of ownership of a corporation.

_____ 20. The most basic form of ownership, including voting rights on major issues, in a company.

_____ 21. The stocks and bonds representing secured, or asset-based, claims by investors against issuers.

_____ 22. A period of rising stock prices.

_____ 23. The electronic trading system that brings buyers and sellers together outside traditional stock exchanges.

_____ 24. An organization of over-the-counter dealers who own, buy, and sell their own securities over a network of electronic communications.

_____ 25. The value of a common stock expressed as total shareholders' equity, divided by the number of shares of stock.

_____ 26. The summary of price trends in a specific industry and/or the stock market as a whole.

_____ 27. An illegal practice of using special knowledge about a firm for profit or gain.

_____ 28. The market in which stocks and bonds are traded.

_____ 29. The specialty index that uses 2000 stocks to measure the performance of the smallest U.S. companies.

_____ 30. The market index based on the prices of 30 of the largest industrial firms listed on the NYSE.

_____ 31. The market in which new stocks and bonds are bought and sold.

_____ 32. The purchase of several different kinds of investments rather than just one.

_____ 33. The relative amount of funds invested in (or allocated to) each of several investment alternatives.

_____ 34. The urrent price of a share of stock in the stock market.

_____ 35. The amount of money that is loaned and must be repaid.

_____ 36. An outside investor who provides new capital for firms in return for a share of equity ownership.

_____ 37. Private funds by wealthy individuals seeking investment opportunities in new growth companies.

_____ 38. The value-weighted market index that includes all NASDAQ-listed companies, both domestic and foreign.

_____ 39. A bond issued by a company as a source of long-term funding.

_____ 40. The fee paid to a lender for the use of borrowed funds, like a rental fee.

_____ 41. The period of falling stock prices.

_____ 42. The failure of the borrower to make payment when due to lenders.

Select the Correct Word
Circle the correct word or phrase in each of the following sentences.

1. Companies sell (stocks) (bonds) to raise long-term funds.

2. The payments to share holders, on a per-share basis includes (dividends) (interest).

3. A stock's real value is in its (book) (market) value.

4. (Primary) (Secondary) markets are where new stocks and bonds are bought and sold.

5. (Discount) (Full-Service) brokers offer a fast, low cost way to participate in the market.

6. In a/an (secured) (unsecured) loan the borrower does not have to put up collateral.

7. The (NYSE) (AMEX) (NASD) is the largest private-sector securities-regulation organization in the world.

8. The highest rating on bonds is (A+) (AAA).

9. (Corporate Raider) (Angel Investor) is an investor conducting a type of hostile takeover.

10. The use of insider trading is (perfectly legal) (totally illegal).

11. (Aggressive) (Conservative) growth funds seek maximum capital appreciation.

12. (Diversification) (Asset allocation) is buying several kinds of investments rather than just one type.

13. A (Bull Market) (Bear Market) is a period of falling stock prices.

14. The DJIA measures performance for (30) (500) (1,500) companies.

Identify the Acronym
To the right of each acronym, give its real name.

1. SEC _____

2. ETF _____

3. ECN _____

4. IPO _____

5. OTC _____

6. NASD _____

7. DJIA _____

8. S&P 500 _____

Identify

In this game, the boxes on the left list items, and the answers are to the right. For instance, "wholesalers and retailers" would be "types of intermediaries." A good exercise would be to get with a fellow classmate. Pretend you're on a game show where you tell the classmate examples, and the classmate furnishes the answers.

Discount brokers and full-service brokers	1. Types of _____ _____
NYSE, AMEX	2. Types of _____ _____
Market value and book value	3. Types of _____ _____
Bear, Bull	4. Types of _____
Common-preferred	5. Types of _____
The Dow, the S&P 500, NASDAQ Composite, Russell 2000 Index	6. Classifications of _____ _____
Secured, Unsecured	7. Types of _____
Corporate, municipal, government, bearer, coupon	8. Types of _____

Learning Objectives—Short Answer or Essay Questions

Learning Objective #1: Explain the concept of the time value of money and the principle of compound growth.

Learning Objective #2: Identify the investment opportunities offered by mutual funds and exchange-traded funds.

Learning Objective #3: Describe the role of securities markets, and identify the major stock exchanges and stock markets.

Learning Objective #4: Explain how securities markets are regulated and tracked.

Learning Objective #5: Describe the risk-return relationship, and discuss the use of diversification and asset allocation for investments.

Learning Objective #6: Describe the various ways that firms raise capital and identify the pros and cons of each method.

Learning Objective #7: Identify the reasons a company might make an initial public offering of its stock, and explain how stock value is determined.

Critical Thinking Questions

1. Why is working capital vital to the firm?

2. Why would a firm consider equity financing as an alternative to debt financing?

Brain Teaser

What is the risk-return relationship?

ANSWERS

True-False—Answers

1. False: The *primary* securities markets involve the buying and selling of new securities, either in public offerings or through private placements (sales to single buyers or small groups of buyers).
2. False: The *secondary* securities market involves the trading of stocks and bonds through such familiar bodies as the New York and American Stock Exchanges.
3. False: Shareholders of *preferred* stock must be paid dividends before shareholders of *common* stock.
4. True
5. True
6. False: The *market* value of common stock is the current price of a share of stock in the stock market.
7. True
8. True
9. True
10. False: A municipal bond is a bond issued by *a state or local* government.
11. True
12. False: A bull market is a period of *rising* stock prices.
13. True
14. True
15. True
16. True
17. False: In a secured loan the borrower guarantees repayment of the loan by pledging the asset as collateral to the lender.
18. True

Multiple Choice—Answers

1. b	3. a	5. c	7. d	9. a	11. b	13. a
2. d	4. d	6. c	8. b	10. c	12. c	14. a

Match the Terms and Concepts with Their Definitions—Answers

1. r	7. x	13. u	19. h	25. i	31. b	37. hh
2. ff	8. ii	14. l	20. gg	26. bb	32. q	38. aa
3. j	9. ll	15. kk	21. a	27. oo	33. mm	39. s
4. nn	10. f	16. pp	22. cc	28. e	34. g	40. jj
5. c	11. p	17. w	23. z	29. v	35. y	41. dd
6. n	12. d	18. m	24. o	30. ee	36.	42. t

Select the Correct Word—Answers

1. bonds	4. primary	7. NASD	10. illegal	13. bear market
2. dividends	5. discount	8. AAA or Aaa	11. Aggressive	14. 30
3. market	6. unsecured	9. corporate raider	12. Diversification	

Identify the Acronym—Answers

1. Securities and Exchange Commission
2. Exchange-Traded Fund
3. Electronic Communication Network
4. Initial Public Offering
5. Over-the-counter
6. National Association of Securities Dealers
7. Dow Jones Industrial Average
8. Standard & Poor's Composite Index

Identify—Answers

1. stock brokers	3. stock values	5. stocks	7. loans
2. stock exchanges	4. markets	6. market indexes	8. bonds

Learning Objectives—Short Answer or Essay Questions—Answers

Learning Objective #1: Explain the concept of the time value of money and the principle of compound growth.

The *time value of money*, perhaps the single most important concept in business finance, recognizes the basic fact that, while it's invested, money grows by earning interest or yielding some other form of return. Time value stems from the principle of *compound growth*—the compounding of interest paid to the investor over given time periods. With each additional time period, interest payments accumulate and earn more interest, thus multiplying the earning capacity of the investment.

Learning Objective #2: Identify the investment opportunities offered by mutual funds and exchange-traded funds.

As an alternative to buying stock, mutual funds and exchange-traded funds are popular because they offer attractive investment opportunities for various financial objectives and often do not require large sums of money for entry. In addition, the simple and easy transaction process makes them accessible to the public.

Mutual funds are created by companies such as T. Rowe Price and Vanguard that pool cash investments from individuals and organizations to purchase a portfolio of stocks, bonds, and other securities. The portfolio is expected to appreciate in market value and otherwise produce income for the mutual fund and its investors.

Learning Objective #3: Describe the role of securities markets, and identify the major stock exchanges and stock markets.

Stocks, bonds, and mutual funds are known as *securities* because they represent *secured*, or financially valuable claims on the part of investors. The markets in which stocks and bonds are sold are called *securities markets*.

Among the stock exchanges that operate on trading floors in the United States, the New York Stock Exchange is the largest. Other, smaller, U.S. exchanges include the American Stock Exchange (AMEX), and several regional stock exchanges located in Chicago, Los Angeles, San Francisco, Cincinnati, and Spokane.

Large foreign exchanges are located in London and Tokyo.

Learning Objective #4: Explain how securities markets are regulated and tracked.

The *Securities and Exchange Commission (SEC)* is the government agency that regulates U.S. securities markets.

Investors use stock indexes to measure market performance and to predict future movements of stock markets. Although not indicative of the status of individual securities, *market indexes* provide useful summaries of overall price trends, both in specific industries and in the stock market as a whole. Market indexes reveal bull and bear market trends. *Bull markets* are periods of rising stock prices, generally lasting 12 months or longer; investors are motivated to buy, confident they will realize capital gains. Periods of falling stock prices, usually 20% off peak prices, are called *bear markets*; investors are motivated to sell, anticipating further falling prices.

Learning Objective #5: Describe the risk-return relationship, and discuss the use of diversification and asset allocation for investments.

The risk-return relationship is the principle that investors expect to receive higher returns for riskier investments and lower returns for safer investments. Individual motivations and tolerance for risk determine each investor's preferred balance for risks versus returns. Diversification and asset allocation are tools for helping investors achieve the desired risk-return balance for an investment portfolio. *Diversification* means buying several different kinds of investments, instead of just one, to reduce the risk of loss if the value of any one security should fall. *Asset allocation* is the proportion of overall money invested in each of various investment alternatives so that the overall risks for the portfolio are low, moderate, or high, depending on the investor's objectives and preferences.

Learning Objective #6: Describe the various ways that firms raise capital and identify the pros and cons of each method.

If a firm needs to raise capital it can turn to borrowing from banks, soliciting cash from private outside investors, or selling bonds to the public. Banks can provide a secured loan to purchase new equipment, but the borrower guarantees repayment of the loan by pledging the asset as collateral to the lender. Outside individuals who provide capital are called angel investors. In return for their investment, angel investors typically expect a sizable piece of ownership in the company (up to 50 percent of its equity). They may also want a formal say in how the company is run. Corporations raise capital by issuing bonds. The bondholder (the lender) has no claim to ownership of the company and does not receive dividends. However, interest payments and repayment of principal are financial obligations; payments to bond holders have priority over dividend payments to stockholders in cases of financial distress.

Learning Objective #7: Identify the reasons a company might make an initial public offering of its stock, and explain how stock value is determined.

Initial public offerings (IPOs)—the first sale of a company's stock to the general public—are a major source of funds that fuel continued growth for many firms, as well as introduce numerous considerations and complexities inherent in running a public company. Going public means selling off part of the company, as private owners lose some control of the company when shares are sold to the public.

There are many factors that affect a stock's value, which in turn affect the value of the business. In addition, different investors measure value differently, and their measurements may change according to circumstance. Investor impact on stock value instead may be based on a long-run perspective considering the company's financial health, past history of results and future forecasts, its record for managerial performance, and overall prospects for competing successfully in the coming years.

Critical Thinking Questions—Answers

1. **Why is working capital vital to the firm?**

   Firms need more than just fixed assets for daily operations; they need current, liquid assets available to meet short-term operating expenses such as employee wages and marketing expenses. The firm's ability to meet these expenses is measured by its working capital: Working capital = Current assets – Current liabilities. Positive working capital means the firm's current assets are large enough to pay off current liabilities. Negative working capital might require the need to borrow from a commercial bank.

2. **Why would a firm consider equity financing as an alternative to debt financing?**

   Equity financing includes either issuing common stock or retaining the firm's earnings. The use of equity financing by means of common stock can be expensive because paying dividends is more expensive than paying bond interest. Retained earnings as a source of capital includes net profits retained for the firm's use rather than paid out in dividends to stockholders. If a company uses retained earnings as capital, it will not have to borrow money and pay interest.

Brain Teaser—Answer

What is the risk-return relationship?

Each type of investment has a risk-return (risk-reward) relationship: Whereas safer investments tend to offer lower returns, riskier investments tend to offer higher returns (rewards). Conservative investors, who have a low tolerance for risk, will opt for no-risk U.S. Treasury Bills, or even intermediate-term high-grade corporate bonds that rate low in terms of risk on future returns, but also low on the size of expected returns. The reverse is true of aggressive investors who prefer the higher risks and potential returns from long-term junk bonds and common stocks.